Ministering In The Secular University:

A Guide For Christian Professors And Staff

Joseph McRae Mellichamp

LEWIS AND STANLEY
3440 Sojourn Drive, Suite 200
Carrollton, TX 75006-2354

Scripture references are taken from the NEW AMERICAN STANDARD BIBLE®, Copyright © 1960, 1962, 1968, 1971, 1973, 1975, 1977, 1995, by the Lockman Foundation. Used by permission.

ISBN: 0-929510-09-7

Library of Congress Catalog Card Number: 97-26127

Printed in the United States of America

To Peggy who has been my true partner in life and in ministry and to Jonathan and Jennifer who were a part of our life in the university.

FOREWORD

MINISTERING IN THE SECULAR UNIVERSITY

As a college or university professor or professional staff member, you are one of the most influential people in our society. And as a Christian professor or staff member, you have great opportunity to impact your students and colleagues, as well as your institution, for the cause of Christ. Yet, as I have traveled around the United States and the world over the past 25 years as a university professor and as National Faculty Representative for Christian Leadership Ministries, I have met few professors or staff members who really are having a significant impact for Christ on their campuses.

I believe that many Christian professors and staff members sincerely desire to make a difference for Christ in the lives of their students and colleagues and on their institution, but they simply don't feel equipped to do so. They don't know what is permissible, what is legal, or what is appropriate. They don't know attractive ways of reaching out to those around them in the university community. And let's face it, most of us are very, very busy. There is not enough time to accomplish all that is necessary to faithfully discharge the duties the institution expects. There certainly isn't time to add ministry involvement in any significant way to what is already required.

If you can identify with any of these statements, this manual is for you. I have been involved as a university professor in Christian ministry on a secular university campus for 25 years. During my time as a professor, I was subject to the same pressures many of you face -- heavy pressure to publish in scholarly journals and pressure to be a good classroom teacher. Throughout my career, I sought to reach out to my students and colleagues in a Christian way, and I tried to have an impact for Christ on my institution. The material presented in this book outlines strategies I have accumulated through years of ministry and represents the *entire* spectrum of ministry opportunities for Christian university and college professors and professional staff.

I personally have used many of the ministry activities presented here and those which I haven't experienced personally, have been used by friends and colleagues at other institutions. These ideas will allow you to have an impact for Christ in your setting that is legal, ethical,

i

appropriate, attractive and effective. By carefully selecting a *few* of these strategies, you can have a significant influence for Christ with only a modest investment of time and energy. In 25 years of ministering on the university campus, I rarely spent more than an hour or two a week in ministry activity. Over the span of a career, an hour or so a week can amount to a significant investment, especially when it is committed to the sovereign hand of the Lord.

I believe that one day, we will stand before God to give Him an account for our service. I further believe that God expects us to have an impact for Him in our spheres of influence. For those of us who work on university and college campuses, that includes the campus -- our students, our colleagues, and the institution. I don't know about you, but I want to hear, "Well done, good and faithful servant," when my service is assessed. Thus, my motivation for ministry was always to be a faithful servant, and my purpose in assembling these materials is to share with you some insights God has given me as I have endeavored to serve Him in the secular university.

I am truly indebted to Dr. Jim Engel and Dr. Walter Bradley for challenging me in the summer of 1970 to begin to think about using my position as a university professor to have an impact for Christ and to many of my colleagues at the University of Alabama over the years since for encouraging me and for participating with me in Christian ministry. For nearly 24 years, there has been a cooperative and, indeed, pioneer spirit among the Christian faculty and staff at the university as we dreamed, planned, and worked together and individually to have an impact for Jesus. I am sure that they join me in challenging you to make a difference. We hope you will find these ideas and materials helpful as you seek to impact those in your university for the Savior.

I also want to thank my daughter, Jennifer Mellichamp, for a thorough job of editing the completed manuscript and to Mike Duggins, Associate National Director of Christian Leadership Ministries, for reading the manuscript and making insightful comments. Finally, I want to thank John Gay of Christian Leadership Ministries for a splendid cover design and Barry Huckaby also of Christian Leadership Ministries for taking care of many of the administrative chores that attend publication of a book.

Rae Mellichamp

MINISTERING IN THE SECULAR UNIVERSITY

TABLE OF CONTENTS

INTRODUCTION

THE SECULAR UNIVERSITY AND YOU

In his book, *The Soul of the American University*, George Marsden describes the decline of Christian thought and influence in the great universities of America -- Harvard, Yale, Princeton, Michigan, Berkeley, Chicago, Stanford -- starting more than a hundred years ago and, for all practical purposes, culminating by the middle part of the 20th century. The *marginalization* of Christianity in the university as Marsden calls it; the gradual, but steady relegation of Christian things to the margins of the university, to the unimportant or trivial regions of the institution. Marsden's book, which ought to be required reading for every Christian university or college professor and staff member in this country, should elicit feelings of embarrassment and deep concern from all Christians, but especially from those who work in the university setting. To be sure, one reason for the demise of Christian thought in the university has been a result of the inability of academics to agree on the appropriate role of Christianity in the university. To articulate such a position is no easy task, but it is assuredly an enterprise we must be about, and it should be an important part of our focus.

Perhaps an even more compelling reason for the marginalization of Christianity in the university is that Christians have simply not been engaged in the fight to keep Christian ideas in the university's marketplace of ideas. Christian professors and, to a lesser extent, staff have stood by and allowed Christianity to be pushed aside often without "lifting a finger" or, more literally, "raising a voice" to oppose what was happening. Those of us in academia might protest that the decline happened and was substantially an accomplished fact before our tenure in the university started, thus we should bear no culpability for it. Yet, in a sense, our generation was the first to come along in the university after the shift occurred, and from this perspective, we are the ones who should have mounted the counterattack. In a way, we have started mustering the troops for the counterattack. That is really the goal of Christian Leadership Ministries -- what can we do as Christians in the university to retake lost ground? What can we do to restore Christian thought to its rightful place in the university?

1

The battle must be fought on two fronts -- an intellectual front and a personal front. The intellectual front has to do with the question of the appropriate role of Christianity in the university. And this action will be waged largely in colloquia, in professional meeting presentations, in scholarly journals and manuscripts, and other such forums. This is certainly an important theater of operations. The battle will be difficult and probably long -- the ground was lost over an extended period of time; we will not likely retake it overnight. The intellectual battle calls for specialized troops, primarily those who deal in the realm of ideas -- the humanities and the hard sciences. The personal front has to do with how we as Christian academics attempt to impact students, colleagues, and, indeed, our institutions for Christ. It has to do with our ministries within the institution as we go about our day-to-day academic activities.

And that is precisely what this manual is about. It is intended to serve as an instruction manual (a manual of arms) for the serious Christian academic concerned about having an impact for Christ in the university. Every Christian professor and staff member should be engaged in operations on the personal front. We have all been charged to be Christ's representatives or ambassadors on a personal level, and we all will give an account of our stewardship in this regard. Those who work in the university who are not engaged at all in any way to impact the institution for the Savior are, to continue the military analogy, derelict in their duty and ultimately will have to answer the charge.

In a talk titled "Giants in the Land," my friend, Dr. Walter Bradley, who is Professor of Mechanical Engineering at Texas A&M University, discusses barriers we must overcome to live a committed lifestyle in the university. One barrier is the opposition. Like the Hebrew spies in Numbers 13:25-14:10 who reconnoitered the land of Canaan at the time of the Exodus, we face well entrenched opposition -- "giants." The university is hostile to Christians. It is not popular to be a visible Christian in the university. To do so is to invite opposition. And quite often, the opposition does not play fair. The playing field is not level. However, recognizing that there assuredly will be opposition, our attitude needs to be like that of Joshua and Caleb, two spies, who proclaimed, "If the Lord is pleased with us, He will bring us into this land and give it to us."

Another barrier we face in living Christianly in the university has to do with approval. To be a visible Christian in the university is to invite the disapproval of those whose approval we seek in much of what we do. The very nature of the research aspect of the university has to do with putting before our colleagues ideas for which we seek approval -- theories, models, approaches, principles. To be successful in research within the university, one must continually have one's ideas subjected to peer review and have these ideas pass muster. Thus, we often become overly concerned about the approval of others. The problem occurs when the distinction between seeking approval for professional contributions and seeking approval for our personal beliefs becomes blurred, as it so easily can. When this happens, our motivation becomes like that of the Pharisees Jesus condemned -- "For they loved the approval of men rather than the approval of God." John 12:43

A third barrier has to do with our attitude concerning whom we serve. It is related somewhat to the issue of approval. As the apostle Paul writes in 1 Corinthians 4:1-4, "Let a man regard us in this manner, as servants of Christ, as stewards of the mysteries of God. In this case, moreover, it is required of stewards that one be found trustworthy. But to me it is a very small thing that I should be examined by you, or by any human court; in fact, I do not even examine myself. I am conscious of nothing against myself; yet I am not by this acquitted; but the one who examines me is the Lord." If we are only interested in serving ourselves, the most expedient approach is the one taken by many; to compartmentalize our life and to practice our Christianity when we leave the university. On the other hand, if we truly want to please the Lord Christ, then we must be found trustworthy in our representation of Him in every sphere of our lives, including the university.

Finally, we must face the issue of persecution. Scripture admonishes in 2 Timothy 3:12, "And indeed, all who desire to live godly in Christ Jesus will be persecuted." If we are truly having an impact for Christ in the university, we can expect persecution. As an old Air Force pilot put it, "If you think you're flying over the target but you're not taking any flack, you'd better check your map because you're probably not over the target." Persecution comes with the turf. However, we don't need to seek it out. If we are wise, if we seek to do things in ways that are legal, ethical, appropriate, and attractive, we will experience commendation and praise more often than we experience persecution. I have tried for most of my professional life to be a bold witness for the Lord in the university, and I can say with complete honesty that though there has been some subtle persecution -- primarily in the form of being avoided by some colleagues -- there also has been a generous share of commendation and praise for the stands I have taken and the service I have rendered.

Ultimately, our attitude about representing Christ in the university must be that it is the right thing to do: Christ has given us this responsibility. The opposition is formidable; we might lose the approval of colleagues; some of us might lose our position in the university; and we will surely experience persecution. For us, the key issue is to be found faithful in doing what the Lord has charged us to do. The outcome is up to God. As Shadrack, Meshack, and Abednego said centuries ago when facing the furnace in Babylon for their faithful service to God, "O Nebuchadnezzar, we do not even need to give you an answer concerning this, if it be so our God whom we serve is able to deliver us from the furnace of blazing fire; and He will deliver us out of your hand, O king. But *even* if He does not, let it be known to you, O king, that we are not going to serve your gods or worship the golden image that you have set up." Daniel 3:16-18

In his best selling book, *The Seven Habits of Highly Effective People*, Stephen Covey challenges the reader to imagine himself on his 85th birthday. Family, friends, and colleagues have gathered to pay tribute. "What would you like for them to say about you on such an occasion?" Covey asks. I had a similar life-defining experience early in my academic career. I remember walking across campus at the University of Alabama one spring afternoon soon after I had joined the faculty as an Assistant Professor there. The trees and shrubs on campus were just beginning to turn green after the winter. Flowers were starting to bloom, birds were flying from tree to tree. As I walked, I reflected on the previous evening when I had read the obituary of a prominent university professor in the local newspaper. This man -- whose name I have long forgotten -- was well-known enough that his obituary started on the front page of the paper and continued on the obituary page. In all, the notice was probably 10 or 12 column inches. Listed were all of his academic accomplishments: his degrees and the universities from which they were obtained; all of the positions he had held in academe; many scholarly publications -- articles, books, monographs; various committee assignments and task force memberships; and much more. There were a few mentions of family: his wife and children, a relative or two. I looked carefully, but saw no mention whatever of anything religious; no mention of a church affiliation, no religious involvement at all, nothing.

As I walked and reflected, it occurred to me that none of the "stuff" he had done was of much use to him then. Now don't misunderstand what I'm saying. For a professor, these things are terribly important. Our research and teaching give us the platform we have as professors. For the Christian professor, this is especially true. If I am not excelling in my research, my colleagues will not be too interested in anything I might have to say about my faith in Christ. If I'm not doing a good job in the classroom, my students are not going to be too excited about my opinions either. So teaching and research are important. But these academic trappings are not the bottom line. They are not and should not be the sum and substance of our lives, which appeared to be the case for the gentleman whose obituary I was considering. As I continued to walk and think, I remember wondering what I would like for my obituary to say about me when my life on earth came to an end. I decided I would want it to say a lot about how I had used my influence as a professor for Christ, to cause students and colleagues to consider Him, to influence the university for good and noble causes.

What about you? What would you like others to say of you at the end of your life? What would have been important for you to have accomplished from a career perspective? Think about when you retire from your university position. Will there be any regrets? Would you do anything differently if you could go back and start over? Wouldn't you agree that taking a stand for Christ in the university would be the most significant thing you could accomplish? If so, why not start now? If you have already started, read on. The material to follow should help you in your effort.

Having faced the giants and determined that we need to push on into the land, let's take a look at the material to be presented. In this manual I have elected to divide the subject matter into three categories: (1) Ministering Individually, (2) Ministering with Others on Campus, and (3) Ministering Nationally and Internationally. There are many, many opportunities for individual Christian professors and staff to have an impact in the university irrespective of what other Christian faculty and staff are doing. For instance, I might look for opportunities in advising situations with my students to suggest spiritual solutions to personal problems where appropriate. It doesn't matter whether I am the only professor on campus seeking to do this or if every other professor is also thus engaged. This is an appropriate thing for any Christian professor to do, and, therefore, I need to be doing it. A number of ways of ministering as an individual in the university are presented in the section "Ministering Individually." There is, furthermore, an opportunity for Christian faculty and staff to work together synergistically to impact students, colleagues, and the institution for Christ. For example, we might work together to bring a prominent speaker to campus to address some segment of the campus population on some topic possibly from a Christian point of view. There are a number of such ways we can work together effectively on campus; several are presented in the section "Ministering With Others on Campus." Finally, Christian professors and academic staff personnel have opportunities to serve beyond just the local campus level; thus, several options for ministry at the national and international level are presented in the section "Ministering Nationally and Internationally."

Before launching ahead into the material on "Ministering Individually," I want to discuss a concept or mindset that has helped me tremendously in the area of ministry and which I think will be helpful as a backdrop for our entire focus on ministry. Figure 1 graphically depicts a "Spiritual Receptivity Continuum." What this diagram suggests is that everyone is to be found somewhere on a continuum in relationship to Christ or Christianity. Everyone to the left of the cross on the diagram is an unbeliever. Unbelievers come in all shades and stripes. Some are openly hostile toward anything religious and especially toward Christianity. Some are simply indifferent. Some are interested; they are actively seeking answers to life's tough questions. People to the right of the cross are believers in the sense of having made a personal commitment of their lives to Christ. Believers also come in all shades and stripes, which we usually measure in terms of Christian maturity. Some believers are baby Christians; some of them have only been Christians for a short while, and some of them have been Christians for years. Some believers, perhaps a very few, are mature Christians. And there are many in between.

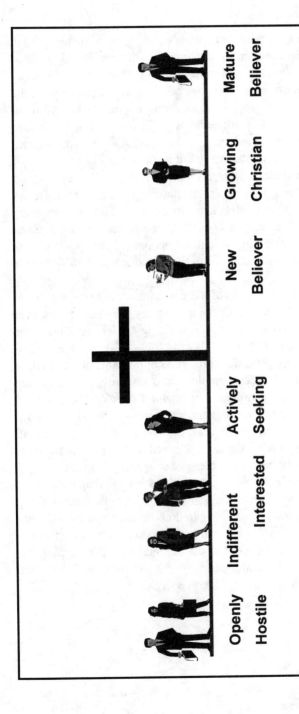

Openly Indifferent Actively Growing Mature
Hostile Interested Seeking New Christian Believer
Believer

Adapted from "What's Gone Wrong With the Harvest?" by James F. Engel and Wilbert Norton, Grand Rapids, Michigan: Zondervan, 1975. Used with permission

Figure 1. Spiritual Receptivity Continuum.

Our job as Christians, regardless of our level of maturity, is to discover where others are on the continuum and what we might do to help move them to the right. Moving people to the right -- that's our charge. There is a term for anything we can do to move someone on the left of the continuum, an unbeliever, toward the cross. We call these activities *evangelism*. For someone who is openly hostile toward Christianity, it might be something as simple as being a friend. It might be helping an international student get accustomed to our culture. For some, it will be sharing a clear presentation of the Gospel with an opportunity to respond. The point is that people are at all different levels in relationship to Christ, and we need to tailor our ministry approach to where they are; a cookie-cutter approach to evangelism won't be as effective as an individualized approach. But, don't get the notion that a Gospel presentation is all there is to evangelism -- there is much, much more.

People on the right side of the continuum, believers, also need to move to the right, to grow in Christian maturity. We need to discover what we can do to help believers move to the right. For new Christians, it might be to help them study and apply the Bible for themselves. For a Christian who has been mired down for years at the same place, it might be to challenge him with the example of our own life. For a mature Christian who is really having an impact for Christ on those around him, it might be a word of thanks or encouragement. There is a term for activities that help believers move to the right on the continuum: we call these activities *discipleship*. Christ challenged us to be in the business of making disciples; we need to be engaged in discipling others.

Moving people to the right! It's a pretty simple concept. Whenever you meet someone, you don't have to muddle around trying to figure out what to do. All you have to do is determine where they are on the continuum and what you might possibly do to help move them to the right. It surely takes the pressure out of ministry. Now, keeping this concept in mind, let's look at some ways we as Christian faculty and staff can minister individually in the university.

PART ONE:

MINISTERING INDIVIDUALLY

Have you ever thought about how unique you are as a university or college professor or staff member? There are only about 550,000 professors in the entire United States. (*Chronicle of Higher Education*, Sept. 2, 1996, p. 24) That's barely two-tenths of 1 percent of the total population of the country. The total number of faculty and staff is about 2,600,000 -- less than 1 percent of the national population. You are indeed unique. And you have a unique opportunity to influence others by virtue of the respect that people in our country accord anyone affiliated with higher education. In public opinion polls ranking the most-respected occupations, *college professor* has always ranked near the top. As a Christian professor or staff member in the university, what kind of impact are you having on students and other faculty and staff at your own institution? What kind of impact are you having as a Christian on your institution?

As I've thought about these same questions, one particular Bible verse has had a profound influence on me. "And you shall be My witnesses both in Jerusalem; and in all Judea and Samaria, and even to the remotest part of the earth." Acts 1:8b In the context, Jesus was speaking to His disciples shortly before His ascension into heaven. Most Christians would agree this verse applies to all disciples of the Lord, not just to those present at the time. As I have reflected on how this command applied to me, it became apparent that the place names -- Jerusalem, Judea, Samaria -- could certainly apply to various spheres of influence, i.e., family, friends, neighborhood, community. And the university surely was one of my spheres of influence. Virtually my whole professional career has been devoted to the area of operations research; efficiency and effectiveness have been objectives of much of my professional work. Knowing intuitively that God is probably efficient and probably values effectiveness, it occurred to me that it would not be very effective for me to spend a lot of time, say 40 to 50 hours a week, in a particular place and not have any influence for Christ there. That just doesn't make sense; it's neither effective nor efficient. It quickly became apparent to me that Acts 1:8 has something to say about what the Lord expects me to accomplish at the university. Among other things such as teaching and research, He expects me to be a witness for Him in the university.

I have spent a great deal of time and energy over the years thinking how I as a Christian professor could have an impact for Christ on my students, my colleagues, and on the institution itself. What I discovered is that the opportunities we have as Christian professors and staff in this regard are practically endless. With a bit of creativity, one can think of dozens of things we can do to have an impact. As I have visited other institutions and talked to other professors and staff members around the world, I have been amazed at the multitude of ways individual Christian faculty and staff are impacting their institutions, their students, and their colleagues for Christ.

In fact, the problem here is not thinking of things to do: it's thinking of things that fit one's personality and abilities, things that one can do in the time available, things that one will feel comfortable doing, things that will attract people to the Savior. In this section, I am going to suggest a number of things that you as a Christian professor or staff member can do from a ministry perspective. You don't have to have any help from other colleagues with these things; they can be done pretty much on your own. One or two of these are really not suggestions -- they really ought to be required. I'll point them out as we go. The other things, though, are truly suggestions. If you see something that appeals to you that you think you would be comfortable doing, and that seems to be a good fit with your situation and circumstances, do it. Go for it!

1. IDENTIFY YOURSELF AS A CHRISTIAN

This is one of those things that ought to be required. You see, we have a huge problem in the university: students come to the university and spend from one semester to four or more (sometimes 10 or more) years and never have a professor who identifies himself or herself as a Christian. Not in class, not in advising situations, not in informal settings, never! In fact, many Christian professors are so afraid they will do or say something "religious" that might offend someone else or, worse still, get them in trouble, they bend over backwards not to let their Christian beliefs or opinions be seen or heard on the campus. The message being communicated more by what is not said than by what is said is *"it is not possible to be educated and also be a Christian."* You might not think this is so. I assure you it is. I have asked many students whether they have ever had a professor identify himself or herself in class as a Christian. The vast majority say no. You might conduct your own experiment if you truly doubt the assertion. Interestingly, when I ask college graduates the same question, recent graduates uniformly respond in the negative whereas those who graduated 20 to 30 or more years ago are more likely to respond affirmatively. The university has changed remarkably in this respect during the last few decades.

Unfortunately, the opposition is not quite as silent on this score as we Christians are. I have had many Christian students tell me of being ridiculed for their Christian faith in class by atheistic professors. Many professors have causes they push in their classes -- feminism, homosexuality, drugs, sex, abortion -- the list is endless. Often the cause has nothing whatever to do with the subject matter of the course, but no matter, the professor has a platform and uses it. The bottom line is that daily, students are being exposed to ideas, philosophies, schemes diametrically opposed to Christianity. They are seeing Christian ideas and ideals questioned, belittled, and ridiculed. It is not at all surprising how effectively the message is being communicated. "There is something fundamentally incompatible with being educated and being a Christian."

So what is the solution? For one thing, Christian professors and staff need to identify themselves to their students as Christians. How?

In the Classroom

Certainly it would be inappropriate to devote significant amounts of class time for a presentation of one's Christian beliefs. However, if you are a committed Christian, your mindset and your approach to your discipline will be influenced to a great extent by your commitment to Christ. In fact, one might argue that you would be doing your students a disservice by not making them aware of your particular perspective. The attitude of the courts generally supports the view that one brings into the classroom one's entire personality, and that in communicating course content to students, a professor will also be communicating other information, including values, beliefs, prejudices, etc.

There are several ways to identify yourself as a Christian in the classroom that, if followed with discretion and good judgment, pass the test of appropriateness and legality.

The First Day of Class. The first class meeting of a course during the semester or quarter is a natural time to communicate to your students that you are a Christian. At least two different approaches have been used successfully in this context:

1. *Qualifications.* Professors often describe their qualifications as part of the course introduction. Consider adding a few personal touches, such as, "I'm Professor Smith. I'll be your instructor in BUS 204 this semester. I have Bachelor's and Master's degrees from the University of Virginia and a Ph.D. in economics from the University of Michigan. I've taught at the university for 20 years. I'm married and my wife and I have two grown children and two grandchildren. You need to know that sometimes in the course I will be presenting my personal perspective of various issues, and my perspective is basically a Christian one."

2. *Introductions.* Sometimes professors begin courses by having each student introduce himself and share some personal information. Consider sharing a brief personal comment of your own along these lines. "I'm Professor Jones. I've taught physics here at the university for 10 years. I want to get to know each of you this semester personally, and I'd like for you to get to know me personally as well. To help you get to know me, let me tell you a few significant things about myself: I have Bachelor's and Master's degrees from the University of Texas and a Ph.D. in physics from the University of Illinois, I'm married and my wife and I have three grown children and five grandchildren, and I'm a Christian."

During the Term. In all but the most technical of courses, there will be a number of natural opportunities during the school term to include a brief Christian testimony. Again, at least two approaches are possible:

1. *In-Class Comments.* Whenever a natural opportunity arises, interject a brief comment as appropriate and continue with the course content. "You're absolutely right, Jon. Profit maximization is not the only acceptable objective for a corporation. There are a number of objectives that firms ought to consider in business operations. In fact, as a Christian, I believe there are a number of very important personnel, environmental, social, and other objectives that firms routinely ignore."

2. *After-Class Discussions.* Students often pose questions not appropriate for class discussions, but tailor-made for after-class consideration. For example, "That raises some very interesting ethical considerations, Jennifer. As a Christian, I have some strong personal views on this issue. If any of you are interested, I'll be happy to stay after class and discuss them with you."

For a classroom situation, brief comments like those indicated above are all that is needed and all that is appropriate. To say much more or to spend much more time than that, would run the risk of imposing on the teacher-student relationship. Your objective in classroom situations is not to share the Gospel or to defend the faith: it is simply to send a message to your students that you are a Christian. Opportunities for in-depth discussions outside of class will come as you are faithful to let students know of your commitment to Christ. It's like Henrietta Mears said, "A Christian should be like the lifeguard at the beach. Everyone on the beach knows who the lifeguard is, but by and large, they go about their activities paying little attention to the lifeguard -- until someone gets in trouble. Then everyone knows where to go for help." Your students need to know of your relationship to Christ. Some of them will get in trouble during their time at the university. They will need to talk to an adult. They will need encouragement. They will need answers to tough questions. How will they know where to turn if you haven't made yourself available?

Some people have objected to the word "Christian," saying that it is not specific enough; it's ambiguous; it's a "loaded" word. "You need to tell them what you mean by Christian. Are you a 'Higher Lifer' or a 'Deeper Lifer' or a 'Fuller Lifer' or what?" they say. My reaction to this objection is (1) when we have been doing nothing along these lines -- which is precisely what Christians have been doing for 50 years -- anything at all is infinitely better than nothing and (2) the objective is to send a signal; those students genuinely interested in pursuing the point will do so outside of class, which is the appropriate place for such discussions.

Optional Sessions. Another way to communicate your faith to your students is during an optional session. There are a number of ways to structure such a presentation.

1. *Life After College.* One effective way to use the optional session is with the "Life After College" talk. I have had undergraduate and graduate students ask me to give them pointers on how to succeed in the business world or in the academic world. It is quite easy to work in just a word of personal testimony along with some other suggestions on success after college. The personal testimony advice can be offered in the context of success being more than just making money or becoming top dog in a company. If the students ask for this, simply be prepared to schedule an optional meeting. If you are initiating the talk yourself, the invitation will be key. You need to let students know in a way that will challenge them to come, but will also communicate that their grade will not be affected in any way by whether or not they come. "We do a good job at the university teaching you how to make a living, but we often neglect to offer you information on how to live. I'd like to share with you some principles I've learned in relating to life. If you're interested, we'll meet in Room 31 Friday at 2 p.m." At the conclusion of the talk, invite anyone who is interested in further discussion to talk privately. Outlines for my "How to Be a Success In Business" and "A Strategy for Academia" talks are included in the following chapter in Exhibit 3-1.

2. *Apologetic.* Another approach for the optional session is an apologetic lecture. Dr. Walter Bradley invites his students each term to a seminar titled "Scientific Evidence for the Existence of God." The seminar is held on an optional basis during the last class period of the

semester. It is followed by an invitation to join Walter for a free lunch during which he shares how and why he became a Christian. In inviting the students, Walter tells them this subject matter is so important he is using the lunch as a "bribe" to get them to come. It is surprising how effective a little tongue-in-cheek honesty can be and how it communicates interest and concern.

3. *Course Related.* With a little thought, interesting course-related optional sessions that have a Christian orientation can be organized. For example, one history professor has developed several optional sessions that explore the Christian beliefs of famous American leaders - - George Washington, Abraham Lincoln, and others. These sessions have been well-attended and provide an excellent vehicle for the group to discuss Christianity in-depth in a non-threatening format.

In Advising Situations

As professors and staff members, we have many opportunities in advising situations to communicate our Christian position to students. Unfortunately, many of us don't take advantage of the opportunities. In my own case, for many years, I thought of academic advising as a necessary, once a semester interruption of time I had blocked out for my research. One day, the Lord convicted me that I was missing out on a ready-made opportunity. As I thought about how to turn academic advising sessions into sharing opportunities, it occurred to me that practically all of our students in the business school are interested in success. Unfortunately, many of them have a very narrow view of success that focuses primarily on making money. I found some attractive Christian literature on "success" that included testimonies of successful businessmen presenting a larger view of success -- one that includes having a personal relationship with God, which ultimately gives life meaning and purpose.

Whenever students came for academic counseling, I would answer their questions and help them map out their academic program. When we had finished and they were satisfied, I would then ask, "Are you interested in success?" Invariably, they would respond with something like, "Well, sure. That's why I'm majoring in business. I want to make a lot of money." I would then give them a copy of the literature and say, "Here is some material on success I think you would enjoy reading in your spare time. It presents a different perspective on success than most people have. It has been helpful to me as I have thought about success. If you have any questions after you've read some of the articles, I'd be happy to talk further with you." For the last several years of my teaching career, most of the undergraduate students I advised received a copy of the literature and an invitation to read about success. What a difference this approach made in my own attitude about advising. Some of my students found an entirely different definition of success as a result.

Of course, students will come to you for various other types of advising. Some advising situations call for spiritual input; some call for wise adult counsel; some should be referred to a professional counselor. As professors and staff, we should be prepared to offer spiritual solutions when the occasion calls for it, even to the extent of sharing the Gospel and offering the student an opportunity to respond to the Lord's invitation. I once had a student who, as a result of my mentioning in class that I was a Christian, came barreling into my office and practically demanded to know how he could also become a Christian. It was pretty easy to lead him through a Gospel tract and see him trust Christ with his life. If you've never thought through the various types of counseling opportunities you have as you interact with students -- which of those could be appropriately turned to a discussion of spiritual issues, and how to do so -- I would challenge you to take the time to prepare yourself now. You will be in for some rich experiences. And be willing to learn from blown opportunities. If a student leaves a counseling session and you are left muttering to yourself, "Wow! I wish I had said this or that." Write down "this or that" and the specific situation and be prepared to capitalize on the next similar opportunity you have.

With Office Decorations

Many of us miss out on one of the simplest ways we have of making a Christian statement to students and colleagues -- through our office decorations. An attractive, attention-getting Christian poster; a strategically placed Bible or Christian book; a well-placed Bible verse can be used effectively to communicate your commitment to Christ to all who enter your office.

For many years, I kept a copy of either the Bible or C.S. Lewis's *Mere Christianity* on my desk. I recall one specific occasion when I was interviewing a young man for a position as assistant professor in the department. As we started the interview, he asked me if I had read Lewis's book. I said that I had and asked him if he had read it, also. He said that he had become a believer by reading it as a graduate student. Well, our interview took an entirely different turn! It turned out that Chuck Schmidt was our top choice for the position, and he accepted the offer we made partly, I'm sure, because of our conversation during his interview and the knowledge that there were other Christians in the department with whom he could fellowship.

One year for my birthday, my wife had my life verse done in calligraphy and nicely framed. I had the verse on the office wall directly beside my desk where it stayed for the remainder of my tenure at the university. I always got a kick out of watching students come into the office, sit down, and survey the pictures on the wall as they waited for me to finish a task so that we could talk. They would look at the old stock certificates that I had had framed and all of my diplomas and other certificates, then the family photos, and finally my life verse. I could see them lean forward to read the verse, then they would sneak a look at me, then look back to the verse. I could imagine them saying to themselves, "Interesting. This guy has a Bible verse on his office wall. Wonder what that means. He must be religious. I'll file this away for future reference."

As you can see, there are many ways of identifying yourself as a Christian to students and colleagues. The issue is not how much you communicate but that you communicate at all. If every Christian professor and staff member in your university or college would follow through on this one issue, we could almost overnight reverse the impression that one can't be educated and also be a Christian.

One final note on this point. I like to think of identifying oneself as a Christian in the context of an event that happened in old pirate movies we used to watch when we were kids (maybe some of us still watch them). You remember the scenario. The good guys would be sailing away on the ocean when all of a sudden, far off on the horizon, a small dot that was obviously a ship would appear. Simultaneously, you would begin to hear bad-guy music -- you know, the sinister kind. But you weren't officially entitled to know these were bad guys -- pirates -- until a very specific event occurred. When the bad guys got almost within cannon range, they would ceremoniously hoist the Jolly Roger, the skull and crossbones, and then immediately start pulverizing the good guys. Then and only then were you, the good guys, and everyone else in the world entitled to know that the bad guys were really bad. This is what we as Christians in the university need to be doing -- in a good sense, of course. We are simply hoisting our colors to let everyone know where we stand. We don't make a big deal of it; if it is in a class situation, we don't take a lot of time with it; it is just a simple declaration of fact for all the world to know. If students or colleagues want to know more about what our position is or how they could also join our side, that is wonderful. If they don't, that's great too. The time might come when they recall our declaration and reconsider.

A few weeks ago, I received a phone call from a businessman in Buffalo, New York. When I answered the phone, he asked, "Is this Dr. Mellichamp?" "Yes it is," I replied. "Dr. Mellichamp, I graduated from the University of Alabama in 1971 and I had you for a course in 1970. You shared briefly in that class that you were a Christian. God used those comments to draw me to Himself and I committed my life to Him shortly after graduation. Every two or three years, I think back over my life and identify the five individuals who have had the greatest impact on my life. You have been in that group for many years and I recently became impressed to get in touch with you to let you know how God used you in my life and how grateful I am for your sharing with us." We chatted for awhile reliving old times and agreed to get together for lunch the next time he is in Atlanta. That call from Bill Crawford was a highlight of my career!

2. MINISTRY TALKS/PAPERS

As faculty and staff in a university or college setting, we often have opportunities to speak to campus audiences on different topics. A variety of such opportunities may arise from time to time, for example, Christian student organizations such as Campus Crusade for Christ, Inter-Varsity Fellowship, The Baptist Student Union, the Wesley Foundation, etc.; other student organizations such as social fraternities and sororities or academic and/or leadership honoraries; athletic teams. The list is practically endless. Often the occasion will call for a talk on a Christian theme; sometimes there will be opportunities to speak evangelistically. Sometimes the talk will be on a secular topic such as leadership or ethics, with an opportunity to interject a brief reference to spiritual things by way of a personal challenge. Unfortunately, we are often unprepared to take advantage of such opportunities, and turn them down for want of time to prepare a suitable talk. We can capitalize on these opportunities, as well we should, with just a bit of anticipation and preparation.

Not all professors and staff necessarily feel called or gifted in the area of speaking -- you might not feel that speaking ought to be a ministry focus for you. I certainly agree, with a couple of exceptions. Let me outline the exceptions first, and then I'll describe all the possibilities in detail. Every Christian (this includes professors and staff) should be prepared to give his personal testimony when opportunities arise. With a modest amount of extra effort, one can expand his testimony into a full-length talk. Another exception is in the areas of grades and time management. If you teach freshmen and/or sophomores, you should seriously consider developing talks that would help your students to succeed in their studies and use of time. What better contribution could you make to your students than to help them succeed in the university?

The Personal Testimony

In 1 Peter 3:15, the apostle writes, "But sanctify Christ as Lord in your hearts, always being ready to make a defense to everyone who asks you to give an account for the hope that is in you, yet with gentleness and reverence." In Mark 5:19, Jesus, after healing a demon-possessed man, said to him, "Go home to your people and report to them what great things the Lord has done for you." It seems clear to me we are to take these passages to mean that, along with other material of an apologetic nature, Christians always ought to be ready to share an account of how they came to know Christ. Unbelievers might argue other proofs of Christianity; it's pretty difficult to argue with someone's experience of the living Christ. This certainly conforms to the admonition to defend with gentleness and reverence. Thus, the personal testimony is a powerful defense of the hope we have as Christians.

A well-written personal testimony that briefly describes your life before you became a Christian, outlines how you became a Christian, and gives some of the changes Christ has made in your life can be expanded with apologetic material into a talk you can use effectively for many speaking opportunities. I routinely give mine, which I call "My Search for Success," to Christian student meetings on campuses, to fraternity and sorority groups, to faculty groups. If you have never prepared your own testimony, I would strongly urge you to do so as soon as possible. If you are not familiar with the technical details of how to write a clear testimony, several Christian organizations including Campus Crusade for Christ and the Navigators have material on how to write a personal testimony. I am including a copy of my testimony in Exhibit 2-1 as an example.

Once you have completed writing your testimony, you might begin to ask the Lord to bring opportunities to share it with others either individually or in speaking situations. I would also encourage you to carry a copy with you in your wallet or purse. I have made this a habit for many years and have had some delightful experiences where I was able to engage individuals in spiritual conversations and leave them with the copy of my testimony to read later. Once, on a plane from Zurich to Warsaw, I struck up a conversation with a Swiss businessman in the next seat. The conversation turned to spiritual issues so I pulled out a copy of my testimony and said, "This is a summary of what I believe. Why don't you read it and then we can talk further?" He put down his *Wall Street Journal* and spent the next 10 or so minutes reading over my testimony. After that, we had an interesting and enjoyable 30 minute conversation about Christianity. He did not make a commitment to Christ, but he left with some clear information on how to if he wanted to do so.

Exhibit 2-1. Personal Testimony.

MY SEARCH FOR SUCCESS

Joseph M. Mellichamp
Emeritus Professor of Management Science
The University of Alabama
Tuscaloosa, AL 35487

I grew up in a family of four sons. As the second son, I have always been an extremely competitive person. As a youth, I felt in order to be recognized, I always had to win, to be the best, to be first in everything. I can remember as a freshman in college thinking about the question, "What can I do to ensure that I will be a success in life?" I decided that if I set high goals for myself and then devoted all my energy to accomplish those goals, I would succeed. So I adopted this as my life philosophy.

My first major goal was to graduate from college with an engineering degree. And I was able to accomplish this, graduating from the Georgia Institute of Technology with a degree in industrial engineering. During my college years, I was an officer in my social fraternity, an editor of the college yearbook, an officer in the Air Force R.O.T.C., and involved in other campus activities. All of this was motivated by my goal-oriented philosophy of life.

During my senior year in college, I married my high school sweetheart. I had always thought it would be nice to have a son and daughter -- in that order. I was so committed to my goal-oriented approach to life that I made this a goal, and my wife and I were able to accomplish it -- a son and a daughter in order.

Upon graduation from college, I served for two and a half years as an officer in the U.S. Air Force. After completing my military service, I accepted a position as an engineer in industry. It was a fantastic job! The company was involved in building a new refinery, and I was able to immediately begin designing equipment and processes to be used in the refinery. I could not have found a more challenging or intellectually stimulating position.

Yet within a few months, I began to have a strange, empty feeling about my life. Whenever I would honestly evaluate my life, I had to admit to myself that something was missing; it just wasn't as fulfilling as I thought it should be. I decided that education was the answer: I needed an advanced degree. So after two years in industry, I left my job and returned to the university to pursue graduate studies.

I was able to complete the requirements for a Ph.D. in engineering management from Clemson University and received an appointment as Assistant Professor of Management Science at the University of Alabama. I thought to myself, "I have arrived! Life is really going to be great from now on." I was not quite 30 years old, and I had achieved every one of the goals I had set for myself. I had an excellent job, a good income, a lovely wife, two fine children, a fine home in a beautiful neighborhood, two cars in the garage and a cocker spaniel in the back yard. I had it all.

Surprisingly, within six months of assuming my new position, the old feeling of emptiness returned. Something was still missing. I couldn't understand it. According to my philosophy of life, I was a success; but when I seriously considered my life, it came up short. As I struggled with this state of mind trying to understand it, it occurred to me that all of the goals I had set for myself were essentially materialistic -- the accumulation of things: degrees, positions, family, money. What if there was a spiritual dimension to life? What if for a person to really be successful, to be fulfilled, one had to come up with answers in this spiritual realm?

These questions lead to others. What if there was a God? What would He be like? I was not much interested in some impersonal force that was somewhere out in the universe impassively observing things. But a personal God who was interested in me; one who wanted to have a personal relationship with me -- I was interested in that kind of God. But how could one find out about God? How could one know Him?

Exhibit 2-1. Continued.

I had always heard that the Bible was God's way of communicating with people. But I had also heard that the Bible was filled with errors and that one had to sort out truth from error. It occurred to me that a sovereign, omnipotent God should be able to communicate with His creation in a reliable, error-free, way, and I began to investigate the Bible seeking to answer the questions, "Is the Bible reliable? Is it true? Can I base my life on what the Bible says about the issues of life?"

The evidence for the reliability of the Bible can be grouped into four areas: prophecy, archaeology, science, and manuscripts. Here is a summary of what I found.

Prophecy. The Bible is a book that is filled with prophetic statements. In fact, it contains hundreds of prophecies -- detailed, very specific prophecies; prophecies about individuals, about people, about cities, about nations, about events, and about governments. In some cases, the time between when a prophecy was made and when it was fulfilled is a thousand years or more. My conclusion was that some power who knows the future and who is, in fact, in control of the affairs of men and nations is responsible for this record.

Archaeology. Much of the archaeological research in biblical lands was initiated by skeptics who were interested in demonstrating that the Bible is inaccurate in details of history and geography. Hundreds of archaeological discoveries over the past 50 to 75 years clearly prove that the Bible is extraordinarily accurate in this regard. One archaeologist has stated, "There is not one single, undisputed archaeological discovery that contradicts the Bible in any point!" My reaction to this type of evidence was that this book clearly merited my consideration.

Science. Having been educated as an engineer, I had been taught that the Bible is not accurate when it touches on what we have learned from science about our world and the universe. But when I began to check into this, I discovered that the explanation offered by the Bible as to how the universe came into existence fits extremely well with what we know from science, and, furthermore, there are numerous details in the Bible about the Earth and the universe that we are just discovering from science. Again, I had to conclude that the Bible was not an ordinary book -- it could not be explained away in ordinary terms.

Manuscripts. One criticism of the Bible I had often heard was that because it was manually copied over and over for thousands of years, there could be little resemblance between the versions we have today and the original version. This sounded like a logical argument to me. Then I learned that texts from the Dead Sea Scrolls (discovered in 1947) dated approximately 200 B.C., had been compared with our earliest previously existing texts dated around 800 A.D. These texts which differed in age by more than 1000 years were described as 99 percent identical!

To me, these evidences for the reliability of the Bible were too much to discount. I had to admit that the only reasonable explanation for the detail, the content, and the accuracy I found in the book was supernatural -- that a sovereign, omnipotent God communicated this word to mankind to reveal Himself and His purposes to us.

What does the Bible tell us about God and his purposes? Briefly, four things: (1) That God loves men and women individually and desires to have a personal relationship with each of us. Apart from this relationship, we can never be satisfied or fulfilled. (2) That we have each rejected God and chosen to live our lives in our own way. This rejection of God is what the Bible calls sin. (3) That God allowed His Son, Jesus Christ, to live and to be executed to pay the penalty for our rejection of God. Jesus rose from the dead that we might have an eternal relationship with God. (4) That we must individually accept God's offer of eternal life by believing what God has accomplished through His Son.

Having considered the facts and found them reasonable, I accepted God's offer through simple faith. That was many years ago. I am still competitive; I still strive for excellence in every area of my life. But I do so realizing that success in life comes from knowing the infinite God of the universe and having a personal relationship with Him. If you have never investigated these issues, I challenge you to do so.

Grades and Time Management Talks

I often ask Christian professors and staff in seminars how many of them would invest several hours a semester (10 hours a year) if doing so would allow them in four years to share part of their personal testimony with 20 percent of the student body in their university or college. This is such an outrageously good deal that almost everyone wants to hear how such a thing could happen. Well, this was my own experience with the "How to Make Better Grades and Have More Fun" talk. Five or six years before my retirement, I found myself teaching graduate courses exclusively, usually very small classes of doctoral students. As I reflected one summer on my career and specifically on how effective I was as a Christian professor in influencing students for Christ, I decided I really wasn't having much of an impact because I didn't have much contact with students.

This realization led me to start seeking ways to have more opportunities to interact with students and particularly undergraduates. At the time, Steve Douglas, a vice president for Campus Crusade for Christ, was giving a talk based on his book, *How to Get Better Grades and Have More Fun*, on many campuses around the country. It was an interesting concept. I thought I could probably give such a talk and that it might come across as well from a professor as from an outsider. I got a copy of Steve's book and read it, and I can honestly say it's a great book -- my wife and I give copies as high school graduation presents. But it wasn't me; I really never used many of the recommendations Steve gives. So I got out some paper and began to make a list of some of the things that helped me as a student. Within 30 minutes, I had an outline for a talk that I have since given more than 100 times to thousands of students. In the first four years at the University of Alabama, I gave the talk about 40 times to approximately 3,600 students (20 percent of the student body averaging 10 hours a year). Of all the ministry things I have done over the years I have been a university professor, this is easily the most enjoyable and rewarding. Helping students in the context of improving their grades is a natural ministry opportunity for faculty. Practically every college student is interested in improving his or her grades, and the prospect of being able to make better grades and have fun at the same time is universally appealing. Here is a venue for reaching college students in a way that addresses felt needs and requires a minimal time investment on your part. If you have never tried this and you think you would enjoy it, or if you are teaching freshmen and/or sophomores, you need to do it. Here's how.

Consider developing and presenting a "How to Make Better Grades and Have More Fun" talk in conjunction with a Christian student group on your campus. Such groups usually sponsor a number of evangelistic programs on campus to develop contacts to share the Gospel one-on-one at a subsequent meeting. One or more of the groups on your campus will probably be delighted to set you up with speaking engagements in dorms, sororities, fraternities, student associations, and other similar student gatherings. They will arrange all publicity for the meeting, make the physical arrangements, and do the follow-up. All you have to do is show up at the appointed time and deliver a dynamite talk on how to make good grades.

The following steps are suggested for getting a grades talk going.

1. Contact your Christian student ministry directors to see if they would be interested. It is likely they will want to have several such talks a year, so you may have to involve some of your colleagues to meet the demand.

2. Obtain a copy of the book *How to Get Better Grades and Have More Fun* by Steve Douglas from Christian Leadership Ministries, 3440 Sojourn Drive, Suite 200, Carrollton, TX 75006-2354. Read the book. It is a fun book to read, and once you start, you won't want to put it down.

3. Using material from the book while drawing from your own experience and sources, develop a 30 to 40 minute talk. When I did my talk, I used things that had helped me as a student; my suggestions are primarily time-management principles, while Steve's are more directed to how to study. Use ideas you can confidently recommend to students.

4. You will only need five or six recommendations. You don't need to cover everything that could possibly improve grades -- just a few heavy

hitters. Each student will be getting a free copy of the book by requesting it at the end of your presentation.

5. Your last point should be a short personal testimony. I use the well-rounded square concept -- that we should seek to develop socially, physically, intellectually, and spiritually. I then share that for many years, I ignored the spiritual dimension of life and thus was never totally satisfied with my life. Remember, you are not trying to present the Gospel in great detail with the students -- that will come later in one-on-one sessions with ministry staff. You are simply using your influence as a professor or staff member to cause them to become open to a consideration of spiritual issues.

6. Develop a handout for your talk. I use a one sheet (front and back) handout that covers the essential points. You may also develop a comment card to get the names, addresses, and comments from students who attend your sessions. Alternatively, the student ministry may already have cards suitable for this.

7. Let the staff know you are ready for business and prepare to have fun.

Several suggestions will be useful as you actually make the presentation.

1. Have a short biographical sketch ready for the staff member or student who will be introducing you.

2. I always like to begin by finding out how many freshmen, sophomores, juniors, and seniors are in the group. You can use this as an ice-breaker, teasing the juniors and seniors by saying that it may be too late for them. NOT!

3. You may suggest to the group that in today's economy, grades are increasingly important in getting a good job after graduation.

4. Try to interact as much as possible. For example, when I cover my point on not cutting classes, I ask how many of them cut a class that day

or that week. Many will respond affirmatively. Then I suggest the two main reasons for unexcused cuts: sleeping in or last-minute studying for an exam or preparing an assignment, neither of which would be necessary if the student was properly managing his or her time.

5. Make your testimony point brief, but effective.

6. At the conclusion of the talk, have two people ready to pass out comment cards and pencils. Ask the students to fill out the cards including their name and address. Then let them know that you would like to give them a free copy of the book, *How to Get Better Grades and Have More Fun*; let them know the ministry staff person will get in touch with them to give them the book if they indicate they want a copy. Ask for their comments on the lecture. I have found it effective to get them to indicate which of my recommendations they will try to implement. Also ask if what you said about spiritual things made sense and if they would like to get together with someone to talk over spiritual issues.

7. Once you have collected the comment cards, thank the students for allowing you to come. Turn the program over to the host.

By way of encouragement, let me share with you my experience with the grades talks at the University of Alabama. I have done the talk in just about every imaginable situation -- for six men in a dormitory, for 150 women in a sorority house, for professional engineering societies, for pledge classes, for the regular Campus Crusade for Christ weekly meeting. When I first started doing the talk, the dorms were essentially closed to Christian ministries; the grades talk has opened the dorms up, and now Christian groups are able to do a variety of other programs as well.

The response has been overwhelmingly enthusiastic. The comment cards are uniformly positive; most students indicate they will implement one or more of my suggestions, about 95 percent ask for a copy of the book and about 5 percent indicate an interest in spiritual things. Of course, each student who fills out a comment card is personally contacted by the ministry staff person and those who are interested have the Gospel, which is printed in the back of the book, presented to them. I have students come up to me on campus frequently thanking me for doing the talk, often sharing how much their grades have improved as a result of the talk.

I have been invited back every year to some dorms and sororities and fraternities. Sometimes, I get a call from someone who has heard about the grades talk from a friend. I always refer these unsolicited calls to a Christian student group which then works with the caller to set up a talk. I am sure that I will never really know the total impact of this effort. I'm convinced that I have impacted the overall student grade point average at the university by a minuscule amount. But the real motivation for the talks is that students are coming to Christ through the follow up of the Christian student ministry staff. Figure 2-1 shows the comment card we use to follow-up students who attend the talk and Exhibit 2-2 is the handout I use for the talks.

**HOW TO GET BETTER GRADES
AND HAVE MORE FUN**

Comments _____

_____

_____

☐ I would like to receive a free copy of the book
☐ I would like to talk more about spiritual things

Name _____

Address _____

_____

Phone _____

Campus Crusade for Christ

Figure 2-1. Comment Card for "How to Make Better Grades" Talk.

Time management is a topic that can also be used effectively for ministry talks. In fact, the grades talk I give is primarily a talk on time management. I think from years of experience that a student can have the best study skills going, but if he is not managing his time properly -- getting up at a reasonable hour, going to class, studying at free times during the day, keeping current in his classes -- he won't be doing that well in his studies. So a good talk on time management

Exhibit 2-2. Handout for "How to Make Better Grades" Talk.

HOW TO MAKE BETTER GRADES AND HAVE MORE FUN

Joseph M. Mellichamp
Emeritus Professor of Management Science
The University of Alabama

Introduction

- Why better grades?
  - Prominent
  - Permanent
- Why Mellichamp?
  - Experience as a professor
  - Experience as a student

Six Easy Principles

- Set a specific GPA goal for college
  - Aim at nothing and you'll hit it every time
  - Monitor progress
  - Take appropriate corrective action
  - Revise your goal downward only as a last resort

- Treat college like an 8 to 5 job
  - Two philosophies
    - Never study before the sun goes down
    - Never study after the sun goes down
  - Two suggestions
    - Get up and get going
    - Make every minute count

Exhibit 2-2. Continued.

- Attend class
  - How many of you cut class today? This week?
  - Correlation between grades and attendance
  - Why students cut class

- Keep up
  - Homework
    - Complete assignments as they are given
    - As soon as they are given
  - Projects
    - Schedule project milestones
    - Leave some slack at the end

- Relate to your professors
  - Treat them like humans
    - One office visit per course per semester
    - Participate in class, be enthusiastic
  - Figure them out
    - What are the course objectives?
    - What will it take to make an A?

- Become a Well Rounded Square

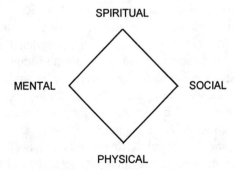

SPIRITUAL

MENTAL   SOCIAL

PHYSICAL

Conclusion

- Do the principles work?
- What about the fun?

principles will minister to most undergraduates and to graduate students, too.

I found this out quite accidentally. I was scheduled to give a grades talk in a women's sorority at a Big 10 school a few years ago. Just before I was to leave home for the campus visit, the person who had set up my speaking engagement called and asked if I would be willing to do a time management talk instead. I scrambled around and modified a talk based on the *Seven Habits of Highly Effective People* that I usually give to faculty and staff and forced it into my grades talk handout format. I showed up at the sorority house to do the talk and discovered that the audience was not a group of sorority women as I had been told, but the president and/or scholarship chairperson of almost every fraternity and sorority on campus. I gave the talk, and the response was amazing. Many of the representatives told me or the person who set up the talk that they would like to have the same talk given to their whole house. I've done the time management talk a number of times since then including in classroom situations and had the same uniformly positive results. Exhibit 2-3 includes the 4 page handout I use with the time management talk.

Christian Leadership has developed a program called *Making the Grade*, which is a combination of a *How to Make Better Grades* talk and a time management talk. *Making the Grade* is a four hour seminar usually lead by a Christian professor; it is available to freshmen and sophomore students for a nominal charge. A variety of materials including overhead transparencies, detailed instruction notes, and a student notebook have been developed for the program by Christian Leadership. Christian Leadership Ministries actually trains professors interested in doing these seminars at several locations around the country. And there is a well-thought out strategy for mailing brochures to students to interest them in signing up for the seminars. Several different ways of communicating spiritual content have been used including offering various materials to students and hosting a pizza party at a subsequent meeting at which the instructor shares his personal testimony. *Making the Grade* may be set up on any campus in the United States by arrangement with the Christian Leadership Ministries office.

Exhibit 2-3. Handouts for "Time Management" Talk.

HOW TO HAVE A GREAT TIME IN COLLEGE

Joseph M. Mellichamp
Emeritus Professor of Management Science
The University of Alabama

Introduction
- Why personal effectiveness?
  - Default
  - Design
- Why Mellichamp?
  - Experience as a professor
  - Experience as a consultant

Six Easy Principles

- Monitor your life goals
  - Write them down
    - Be specific
    - Include every area
  - Be accountable for them
    - Develop an accountability checklist
    - Enlist an accountability partner

- Control your time
  - Classify activities
    - Urgent vs. not urgent
    - Important vs. not important
  - Use calendars
    - Weekly
    - Yearly or six-month
  - Learn to say NO
  - Be flexible

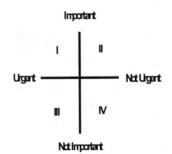

Exhibit 2-3. Continued.

- Treat college like an 8 to 5 job
  - Two philosophies
    - Never study before the sun goes down
    - Never study after the sun goes down
  - Two suggestions
    - Get up and get going
    - Make every minute count

- Use technology
  - Computer
  - Internet/E-mail
  - Telephone

- Organize your workplace
  - File maintenance
    - Use it or trash it
    - Make files map your roles
  - Paper processing
    - Handle it once
    - Do it now

- Become a Well-Rounded Square

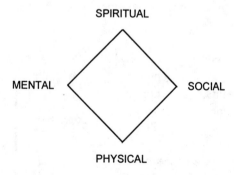

Conclusion

Exhibit 2-3. Continued.

JOHN STUDENT
Life Goals

Academic

• Long Range

    - To obtain a B.S. in industrial engineering
    - To graduate with honors. Overall GPA target: 3.5
    - To pursue graduate studies, possibly an MBA

• Short Range

    - To make the Dean's List every semester
    - To approach my studies like an 8 to 5 job

Social

• Long Range

    - To enjoy the social aspects of my university experience
    - To develop several quality friendships with men and women
    - To look for my future wife

• Short Range

    - To have at least one social engagement each week
    - To be an active, contributing member of my social fraternity
    - To try to develop in one or more social areas; e.g., manners,
      conversation skills

Spiritual

• Devotions. To have quality, consistent daily devotions
• Campus Crusade. To attend weekly meeting faithfully

Physical

• Exercise. To run 2 to 3 miles three days a week
• Diet. To maintain weight, cholesterol, and blood pressure

34

Exhibit 2-3. Continued.

Weekly Schedule
John Student

Roles	Goals
Academic	
IE 424 quiz	Review 2 hrs
IE 415 report	Outline
FI 410	WSJ Article
Social	
Frat Dance	Get date
IFC Track	5k Run

Appointments/Commitments

Today's Priorities

	Sunday 4/21/96	Monday 4/22/96	Tuesday 4/23/96	Wednesday 4/24/96	Thursday 4/25/96	Friday 4/26/96	Saturday 4/27/96
		Run @ 6:30		Run @ 6:30		Run @ 6:30	
8:00		IE 424		IE 424		IE 424	
9:00			IE 423		IE 423		
10:00		IE 415		IE 415		IE 415	
11:00	CHURCH						
12:00	LUNCH	LUNCH	LUNCH	LUNCH	LUNCH	LUNCH	LUNCH
1:00		AC 403	FI 410	AC 403	FI 410	AC 403	
2:00		PSY 451		PSY 451		PSY 451	
3:00							
4:00							
5:00							
Evening				FRAT MEETING	CCC WEEKLY MEETING		

Sharpen the Saw

Physical	Run 3X/Week
Mental	2 Bks/Month
Spiritual	Devotions
Social	Frat Dance

Other Ministry Talks

Of course, there are many other ministry talk possibilities for those of you who enjoy speaking and who see such opportunities as a good ministry option. Some years ago, Walter Bradley put together a talk titled "Scientific Evidence for the Existence of God" in which he looks at a variety of evidence from physics, chemistry, and other disciplines that led him to conclude the universe was *designed*; it couldn't have just happened. Walter has given this talk on dozens of campuses in the U.S. and abroad to thousands of students, faculty, and others. My colleague at the University of Alabama, Phil Bishop, has a talk, "Fearfully and Wonderfully Made," in which he shows how the marvelous complexity of the human body argues for the existence of intelligent design. Phil has given this talk in optional class presentations, as well as in a variety of other settings. Fritz Schaefer, Professor of Computational Chemistry at the University of Georgia, has a talk titled "Stephen Hawking, God and the Big Bang," which he has given frequently to enthusiastic audiences.

Do you have a particular interest that could be developed into a similar ministry talk? It might be that you've done a lot of reading in the area of creation and evolution. Perhaps you have developed skills in the area of financial management based on scriptural principles. If so, it probably wouldn't take much effort to take that interest and develop it into a full-blown talk. If you do, be prepared to have some rich experiences as you take it on the road.

3. DISCIPLINE PAPERS/TALKS

University professors have a wonderful opportunity to identify themselves to both students and colleagues through various *discipline* papers and/or talks. Unfortunately, only a few professors take advantage of these opportunities due primarily to a lack of preparation. Discipline papers/talks are related to the academic discipline of a professor and may be classified into three major types: *position* papers, *issues* papers, and *success* papers. For ease of communication, I'm going to use the term paper in this chapter to refer to either an oral presentation (talk) or a written paper, the assumption being that a paper would be created first, and a talk might result from a paper.

Position Papers/Talks

One exercise every Christian professor should complete is to integrate his Christian worldview with his academic discipline. That is, one should think through and commit to writing the implications of a Christian worldview in one's discipline. How does the Christian worldview resonate with the discipline? What are the tension points between the Christian worldview and the discipline? How does Christianity impact one's academic discipline and/or how does one's academic discipline impact Christianity? How does one's academic discipline impact the culture? How does Christianity impact practitioners of the discipline? What unique opportunities does the discipline present Christian practitioners of the discipline? Every Christian professor should carefully think through his discipline and answer these and a host of similar questions. The difference between *the Christian who happens to be a professor* and *the professor who happens to be a Christian* can be measured by how well one has thought through these issues and come up with meaningful answers.

The professor who has faced the task of integrating his faith with his discipline will understand how he can impact students, colleagues and the institution through the practice of his discipline. Bob Brooks, a finance professor friend at the University of Alabama, has developed a comprehensive document showing what the Bible teaches about money and the use of money. He has had many opportunities to give talks based on the paper in a variety of settings, including academic ones. Phil Bishop's talk, "Fearfully and Wonderfully Made," is actually a discipline talk -- it grew out of Phil's examination of his discipline, human physiology, from a Christian perspective. A number of years ago, I presented a paper titled "The *Artificial* in Artificial Intelligence is *Real*" at an international symposium that addressed the question, "Is the human mind more than just a very fast, very sophisticated computer?" To write the paper, I had to carefully think through the field of artificial intelligence from a Christian point of view. However, since the symposium was a secular enterprise, the arguments had to be made entirely from a secular frame of reference; I could not resort to biblical arguments. I have presented this talk numerous times since the original symposium in academic settings and have had many fruitful discussions as a result of doing the research.

Christian Leadership Ministries is in the process of collecting examples of position papers from various disciplines. These are available from the Christian Leadership Ministries Website -- http://www.leaderu.com.

Issues Papers/Talks

The *issues* paper is similar to the position paper in that it focuses on a particular academic discipline; it differs from the position paper in the sense that it isolates a single issue within the discipline. An issue that crops up in practically every discipline -- even the most sterile ones -- is the issue of ethics. Many academic programs, departments, and colleges are attempting to integrate coverage of ethics into their curricula. To have professors voluntarily integrate and treat ethical issues in their courses is seen by most administrators as a good thing. Now, the wonderful thing about ethics is that there is no honest way of discussing the topic without identifying the sources of ethical standards, and one of the primary sources of ethical standards is religious writings. Many textbooks on ethics will have a section or chapter covering the various sources of ethical standards -- religious writings will be mentioned as a primary source. Once the subject of religious writings is introduced into the discussion, it is a simple matter to suggest that for a Christian, the Bible is a primary source of ethical standards.

In 1989, I was invited to write a chapter in a book being edited by Richard Chewning, Chavanne Professor of Christian Ethics in the Hankamer School of Business at Baylor University. The title of the book is *Biblical Principles & Business: The Practice* (Colorado Springs, CO: Navpress, 1990). The title of my chapter is "Applying Biblical Principles in Information Systems and Operations Research." To write this piece, I had to identify the various ethical issues in two major areas of the business enterprise, i.e., information systems and operations research, and to show how the application of biblical principles might mitigate ethical violations in these two areas. Doing the background research necessary to write the chapter is one of the most productive things I accomplished in my academic career; I have had many opportunities to present all or parts of this work primarily in academic settings. As a matter of fact, I used the paper as a lecture in most of my graduate courses to launch discussions of ethical considerations and to identify myself as a Christian to my students. In business administration, an issues paper in the area of management principles can easily be developed. Some years ago, the late Carl Sagan published an interesting article in, of all places, *Parade Magazine* titled, "Rules to Live By." [Nov. 28, 1993, pp. 12-14] His paper is especially helpful in introducing a discussion of the place of religious sources in ethical systems. In this piece, Sagan starts with The Golden Rule, which happens to be the most commonly employed management principle in the workplace, and proceeds through a series of other rules to show that what he calls "The Gold-plated Brazen Rule" is actually the preferred rule to use in relating to others. What Sagan fails to realize (or to disclose) is that this rule is actually a special case of the Golden Rule. I have used Sagan's little article on a number of occasions to talk about managing employees in the workplace. It is a fun exercise to go through his rules with students and to give examples of when the different rules would be advantageous.

Success Papers

We discussed the topic of *success* talks in the chapter on "Identify Yourself as a Christian." I have generally used two approaches to these talks, depending on the particular audience. For an undergraduate class, the "How to be a Success in Business" talk works well. It certainly answers some important questions students who are facing the prospect of entering the workplace for the first time have. This approach would also be suitable for an MBA class. For classes consisting primarily of doctoral students aspiring to become university and college professors, "A Strategy for Academia" is a good approach. Outlines for both of these talks are included in Exhibit 3-1. You can see from the outlines how I bring spiritual issues into the talk. I merely suggest that spiritual considerations are important and should be taken into account as one pursues success. Again, my purpose is not to share the Gospel. It is just a reminder and a challenge to consider the spiritual dimension of life. I have given both of these lectures in classroom

Exhibit 3-1. Handouts for "Success" Talks.

HOW TO BE A SUCCESS IN BUSINESS
Joseph McRae Mellichamp, Ph.D.
Emeritus Professor of Management Science
The University of Alabama

Develop a Game Plan for Your Career/Life
- Take time to plan and evaluate.
- Set goals and objectives. "If you aim at nothing, you will hit it every time."
- Set priorities. Important things vs. urgent things.

Have a "Can Do" Attitude
- Anticipate what is expected of you.
- Accept every assignment with enthusiasm.
- Be flexible.
- Come early, stay late.
- Never violate your personal code of ethics.

Aim for Excellence in Every Task
- "It just takes a little extra effort to go first class."
- Earn a reputation for excellence.

Look for Career-Making Opportunities
- Too risky or too difficult for others.
- Actively seek greater responsibility.
- Don't be afraid to fail. Failure is rarely fatal.
- Learn from your mistakes.

Relate Properly to Others
- "Don't call H.Q. until the enemy is coming through the front door."
- "Three ways to do things: the right way, the wrong way, the boss's way."
- Never correct your superior in public, and rarely in private.
- Don't draw attention to your weaknesses.
- "There is no such thing as a personality conflict."
- Be better than your peers, but don't show them up.
- Help your subordinates succeed.

Pay Attention to Politics
- Understand office politics, but don't participate.
- "Make your points in the trenches, and attend the parades."

40

Exhibit 3-1. Continued.

Pay Attention to Your Image
- Dress for success.
- Keep yourself physically fit.

Have a Purpose Larger than Your Job

A STRATEGY FOR ACADEMIA
Joseph McRae Mellichamp, Ph.D.
Emeritus Professor of Management Science
The University of Alabama

Set Specific Long-range/Short-range Objectives
- Research
  - Long-range: Become nationally known in an area.
  - Short-range:
    - Two articles per year in target journals.
    - One to two presentations per year.
- Teaching
  - Long-range: Reputation for excellence.
  - Short-range: Consistently good evaluations.

Specialize
- Research: One main area.
- Teaching: One or two courses.

Things to Avoid
- Committee work. Do your share, no more.
- Preparations. The fewer the better.
- Politics. Understand, but don't participate.
- Administration. Unless you want a career.

Become a Manager
- Of activity. You think, let others work.
- Of time. Do important things, not urgent things.

Become a Well-Rounded Square
- Mental
- Physical
- Social
- Spiritual

situations, mainly on requests from students, and have received positive feedback.

4. MINISTERING TO STUDENTS

As Christian professors and staff members in the university, we have many opportunities to minister in a significant way in the lives of students -- our own students in particular and other students as well. Unfortunately, not many of us are taking advantage of these opportunities. In my 25 years on the faculty at the University of Alabama, I knew of only a few professors and staff members who had any kind of Christian ministry on campus with students. And from the traveling I've done to many other campuses, I believe this true in general. When I think of the great opportunity we have as Christian faculty and staff to influence young lives for good and when I realize how little advantage we have taken of our opportunity, I am saddened. If you are already ministering to students in your university setting, that's wonderful. Perhaps the material that follows will give you some new ideas. If you haven't been ministering to students, perhaps you are at a point where you would like to begin to reach out. Let me share a number of possibilities with you. The different ways of ministering to students I will be describing vary dramatically in terms of the amount of time necessary, so be sure to count the cost carefully before proceeding with one of these suggestions.

Bible Studies

Perhaps the most common way of ministering to students would be to lead a Bible study for some student group. The group might be some subset of your own students or it could consist of students other than your own. Of course, if you are a staff member, the students will most likely not be your own. Some professors have trouble with the idea of leading a Bible study involving their own students, but having done so for a number of years, I can assure you that with a modicum of care, it can be done without posing any conflict of interest at all. I'll share one personal experience, and then we'll come back to this point.

A number of years ago, I was asked by several law school students to lead a Bible study for them. They had met me either through my involvement with Campus Crusade for Christ or through my church. Frankly, I was flattered, first, because my reputation as a Christian had apparently spread beyond the business school and, second, because they were graduate students in a very demanding curriculum -- their commitment attracted me. So I readily consented. Every Thursday for a year, I would leave the business school at lunch, get in my car and drive across campus to the law school, to lead this Bible study. I don't remember too much about the specifics of the study; I am still in touch with some of the men who were involved, and it apparently had an impact on them. What I do remember was what transpired as a result of my participation.

One day as I was walking out of the business school to my car, I had a thought. It was almost as if the Lord tapped me on the shoulder and said, "What's the matter, Mellichamp? Aren't there any graduate students in the business school who would like to be involved in a Bible study? Why are you going all the way across campus to minister to someone else's students? That's not really very efficient or practical." Well, this made a pretty profound impression on me, and I started praying about and planning a Bible study for MBA students beginning the following fall semester. In the first few weeks of the semester, I noticed that some of the students who had been involved in Campus Crusade for Christ as undergraduates the previous year were in my first semester MBA class. I asked them to stay after class one day and after the room had cleared, asked if any of them would be interested in a Bible study that I might lead. To my astonishment they said that several of them had already talked about having a study and would be overjoyed if I would lead it.

We started meeting one night a week in our home which was conveniently located less than a mile from campus. This occurred in the 1982-83 school year. I led the MBA Bible study for several years until I started teaching doctoral students almost exclusively. As I phased out of MBA teaching, Bob Brooks, a young finance professor took over, and the MBA study is still in existence today. At times, we had as many as 10 percent of the entire MBA class at Alabama involved in the study! Once, when we were considering principles of administration from the book of Nehemiah, some of the students shared in a case discussion in one of their classes, how some of the principles we had covered the night before in the Bible study applied to the case. What an impact that must have made on their classmates and the professor!

One of the possessions I have that I truly cherish is a cross-stitch rendering of one of my favorite expressions that Roby Gill's wife, Karen (who was also a member of the study), made for me. The students had it framed, and they all signed the back and gave it to me for their graduation. David Owen wrote, "My life has truly been blessed by having met you. Hopefully I can pass this on to those I meet in the future. Thanks for everything." Today, he is in business and remains a close personal friend. Patte Trimm wrote, "It takes someone very special to take the time to care. Thanks." I guess it's pretty easy to see why I was involved in this way. I had the opportunity to lead some of these students to faith in Christ privately, others were encouraged in their faith and began to think for perhaps the first time about being a Christian in the business world. Of course, I had to be careful not to let their role in the Bible study affect my evaluation of their classroom performance. In fact, if anything, I was a bit harder on them because as Christians, I expected more out of them. And I suspect they knew this. I had no problems with familiarity, which I think might be a concern of some professors. The men and women always were very respectful and careful about how they addressed me.

Sometime earlier in my career than the MBA study, my wife and I started a Bible study for international students. Peggy was teaching English as a Second Language to internationals and their wives through one of the local churches and so she had plenty of contacts with internationals and, of course, I had numerous contacts through the business school. At any rate, we invited a bunch of them to come to our home one night a week for a survey of the Bible that I would lead to give them a first-hand idea of what many Americans believe. This study lasted for several years, and we had a grand time. For many of these students it was the only opportunity they had to go into an American home. For others, it was their first exposure to Christianity. I recall one student telling me that his professor at home had severely warned him before coming to the States, "There are two things you don't discuss with Americans: politics and religion." There's no telling how many international students come here with that same admonition and, thus, fail to ever gain any exposure to the religious side of American life.

I don't recall specifically any of these students coming to faith in Christ, but I am confident that they moved to the right significantly on the spiritual receptivity continuum. I do know that after perhaps 20 years, several of them still write Christmas letters every year, sometimes in very broken English, to our "Dear Dr. Mellichamp and Peggy." One year while the International Student Bible study was going on, we decided to invite all of them with their spouses and children for Thanksgiving dinner. Of course, none of them had ever had an American Thanksgiving dinner before. Peggy got some big aluminum foil pans from the store and cooked turkey and dressing, green beans, rice and gravy, sweet potato soufflé, and pumpkin pie -- the whole works for about 30 of them. We had a great time. I gave a little explanation of why we celebrate Thanksgiving, we thanked the Lord for the feast, and then we plowed into all of that food. They talked about the meal for months and were disappointed when we couldn't do it again the following year because of family travel commitments.

I'm sure it was during this time when we had so many international students in and out of our home that our son and daughter began to get interested in internationals as well. They would have both been in junior high school about this time. Both have since done short-term missionary projects -- Jonathan on the Amazon River in Brazil and Jennifer in Japan; Jonathan was involved with Campus Crusade for Christ's *JESUS* film project team traveling internationally for several years. We have all been hooked on international travel since those early days of my career and I'm convinced that the International Student Bible Study played an important part in shaping our thinking along these lines.

You can probably tell I am big on student Bible studies. This is a fairly time-intensive activity, though, requiring about 1 1/2 to 2 hours per week for the actual meeting and perhaps another hour of preparation. It's probably best to meet in a home if possible, thus, it would be helpful to live close to campus. All students -- undergraduates, graduates and especially internationals -- like to occasionally get away from campus and into a "real home." If a home study is not possible because of distance, try to meet on campus, perhaps in the student center or a conference room. I have had small

Bible studies from time to time in my office, and that works well. It's just an added plus to have the meeting in your home.

If you decide to give this a go, a couple of suggestions are in order. First of all, start praying about it and ask the Lord to lead you to students who would be receptive to the idea. Then, begin to think about a particular target group. Perhaps you have a number of graduate students who work in your lab; maybe there are several international students in your college; perhaps you have a number of seniors in your program area. You might approach one or two of the key students and let them do your recruiting for you. Finally, you need to pick a topic that will have some relevance for them. This shouldn't be too difficult, but might require a bit of digging on your part to put together an interesting study -- a task that will be beneficial for you. This could be the beginnings of a position paper in your discipline.

Video Discussion Series

Walter and Ann Bradley, who have ministered together effectively as a faculty couple for more than 30 years and have pioneered many ministry strategies, deserve grateful credit for thinking of and implementing the Video Discussion Series, or as they call it -- "Friday Night at the Movies." Americans like to watch movies. So do internationals. Ditto for college students. Students also like to eat. Several years ago, Walter had the idea of linking these two peculiar habits of students in a discussion-series format. He and Ann began inviting students to their home for a pizza dinner followed by a video movie. After watching the video, Walter would lead an informal discussion of issues raised by the video. Over time, they worked out the format of Friday Night at the Movies. Now, every semester, they invite his students to three to five Friday-night sessions featuring such movies as: *Chariots of Fire*, *Citizen Kane*, *Crimes and Misdemeanors*, and *Out of Africa*. The discussions following the movies have been natural and engaging; students have felt free to voice their personal beliefs and to consider Christian positions put forth by Walter and Ann.

If this seems like a huge undertaking to you, try it once for one Friday night. I think you will be hooked and will want to continue at some level for a long time to come. My last year at the University of Alabama, Peggy and I decided to try this with some international students with whom we were cultivating relationships. We had five graduate students from the People's Republic of China to dinner, after which we watched *Fiddler on the Roof*. At the conclusion of the movie, the students bombarded us with questions about the film. We talked for almost an hour about the Jewish culture, traditions, the differences between Judaism and Christianity. And the discussion could have gone on much longer, but by then, it was quite late, and we decided to cut things off. Several weeks later, one of these students called Peggy to ask if she could discuss a personal problem with her. The problem was, of course, a symptom of spiritual need; Peggy was able to share the Gospel with her, and she trusted Christ. I don't think this would have happened apart from our discussion after the movie.

David Veerman has written a book, *Video Movies Worth Watching* (Grand Rapids, MI: Baker Book House, 1992), that is useful for selecting good videos for this ministry approach. The book reviews 83 different movies, giving the following information for each movie: rating, length, date of release, synopsis and review, suggestions for viewing, important scenes and/or quotes, discussion questions, outline of talk or wrap-up, and related Bible references. With a copy of Veerman's book, some students, a few pizzas, and a Friday night, you'll be in for a fun and significant evening.

Lunch with the Professor

Several years ago at our National Faculty Leadership Conference in Colorado, a marketing professor shared an interesting idea for getting to know students better and for letting them know you are a Christian. He decided to see whether any of his students would be interested in having a one time, Dutch-treat lunch with him for the purpose of chatting informally. The ground rules were that you couldn't talk about the grade you made on the last exam or what would be on the next exam -- anything that would take advantage of the situation was ruled out. But anything else was OK. How the football team was doing, the Super Bowl, the stock market, anything. So he made the proposal to the class and passed around a sign-up sheet for anyone who was interested, thinking he might have a few takers and that he could devote one lunch a week for the remainder of the term to a student or two. Major tactical mistake! He was totally unprepared for the response. It was a large class with nearly 100 students, and every single student in the class signed up for lunch! He ended up meeting a couple of days each week for the rest of the term with three to four students.

This is a great illustration of how interested students are in their professors and how much they look up to and respect them. How would you ever use such a situation to communicate your faith in Christ? Simple. When you sit down to eat, say something like, "Men and/or women, as a Christian, I always like to thank the Lord for my food and ask Him to bless my meals, so if you'll bow with me, I'll do that now." After you have returned thanks, you can turn to the students and thank them for coming. Then ask them what they would like to talk about. If the conversation returns to spiritual issues, wonderful; if it doesn't, that's wonderful too. You have already sent a clear message of where you stand. Although I've never tried this approach, it seems like it would be a great way to get to know students a little better than you could just through classroom interaction. I think it would open up some additional ministry opportunities with some of the students.

In Your Home

My wife and I were married after my senior year in college and after her freshman year. She followed me around during the early stages of my career trying to finish up her education and after 10 years, two children, and six universities, she managed to get her degree. You could certainly say she was well-traveled. One of the highlights of her college experience occurred in her second senior year (she had to change majors a couple of times as she moved from school to school) at Clemson University. At the end of the spring semester, one of her English professors had his entire class and their spouses over to his home for a late afternoon reception. Apparently, he did this every semester for all his classes. That event took place more than 30 years ago, yet it is still a vivid memory for Peggy and me. It was the only time in Peggy's undergraduate days when a professor opened his home to his students. I *never* had a professor in my undergraduate career do this, and it happened only three times in my graduate career. We don't know whether he had the reception to reach out as a Christian to his students; it's possible, though there was no indication. Apparently, he

48

did this because he cared for his students, and he wanted to do something special for them. Wow, did it ever have an impact!

Want to do something special for your students that will communicate to them you are interested and care for them? Try having them over to your home for some occasion. Many of us are afraid of doing something like this because we want everything to be perfect. It's never going to happen. I remember our first experience in this regard. It was the first graduate class I taught at the University of Alabama. We were living in a large rental house with mostly "early attic" furniture. At that time, the university had a large population of military officers in its graduate programs. I had a full colonel and a slew of lieutenant colonels, majors and captains in my class -- people who probably lived in much nicer quarters than ours. It was cold -- February. Thirty minutes before the students and their wives (I didn't have female students in those days) were to arrive, the main water pipe into the house burst. We did the whole evening *sans* water. You know what? No one cared. They were so delighted to be able to spend some informal time with me and to meet Peggy, that they couldn't have cared less. I'm still in touch with some of those first students and that evening was memorable for them. Unfortunately, at the time, Peggy and I were just beginning to grow as Christians, and I had never even thought of having a Christian influence with my students. Interestingly, God has given me a second opportunity with some of those same students! I started doing consulting work for one of them, Larry Fillmer, several years later. As we worked together, Larry shared with me that he had trusted Christ shortly after his stay at Alabama during a family crisis. He and I have remained in close contact over the years and he is an enthusiastic supporter of our ministry.

During the course of my career at the university, we have used our home extensively in ministering to students. We have had my classes over for dinner. I have held class there. I have had Bible studies there. We have had hundreds of international students and their families -- moms, dads, aunts, uncles, cousins -- there for dinner, for tea, for coffee, for dessert, as house guests at graduation. We've had students spend a night or two as a getaway to study for exams. We've had leadership receptions for Christian student groups there. You name it, and we have probably done it if it concerns opening up one's home to students. On many of these occasions, we have intentionally tried to share something about our relationship with Christ with the students; perhaps something as simple as saying, "We are delighted to have you in our home. As Christians, we are thankful to the Lord for the many ways He blesses us. Let's pause now before eating and thank Him for the food and for the fellowship we will have together." Often, we were just being hospitable. I don't ever want to hear of an international visitor coming to this country and not being invited inside an American home; sometimes, that has been our only motivation.

I suppose if I have one regret in this respect, it would be that we did not start early on having every one of my classes over to the house at least once for the purpose of showing that we cared for them and to identify ourselves as Christians. And I have only myself to blame for this because Peggy certainly encouraged me to do this. It's too late for me. What about you? This is such a simple thing to do. It takes perhaps two hours for the event and a couple of hours to prepare. Having experienced being "at home with the professor" from both sides, I can guarantee you some memorable experiences.

Christian Student Ministries

During my first semester at Alabama, we were encouraged by my brother-in-law, Barry Huckaby, to get in touch with the Campus Crusade for Christ staff on campus. Peggy did some calling around, and we finally located Rick and Laurel Langston, the campus directors of the student ministry. In January 1970, we met them for coffee. They told us later they had been praying for professors to be involved in the ministry. At the time, on the spiritual receptivity continuum, Peggy and I both were glued to the base of the cross. Were we ever BABY Christians! Neither of us had grown at all beyond simple commitment of our lives to Christ years earlier. Rick must have recognized this because he challenged us to go through the standard training courses that all the Campus Crusade for Christ students undertake. Then, it was called Leadership Training Course (LTC) -- Basic, Intermediate, and Advanced. Well, I imagined myself as a leader, so we consented to do the training and it was probably the best decision I've ever made next to trusting Christ.

We attended one night a week for a year and a half with all the Campus Crusade for Christ students -- freshmen, sophomores -- all of them. Jonathan and Jennifer were in grammar school then, and they went with us. They would sit in the back of the class and do their homework and then read comic books, color, or whatever. And they loved it. The college students made a big deal over them and, of course, the children thought the college students hung the moon. All the while, Mom and Dad were learning about assurance of salvation, the Spirit-filled life, how to share the *Four Spiritual Laws*, how to have a quiet time, how to write our personal testimony -- all of the Campus Crusade for Christ basics. By the end of that year and a half, we were pretty well along on the path to spiritual maturity. If you have never been really grounded in the basics of the Christian faith, I would heartily recommend that you waste no time in getting the job done. You don't have to sit with freshmen to do so, Christian Leadership Ministries has training packages for faculty and staff to enable you to mature in your faith, and your church probably also has excellent programs as well.

What does all this have to do with "Ministering to Students?" Just this. I don't know of a Christian student ministry that wouldn't be overjoyed to have mature Christian professors and staff participating with them on the campus. How? Well, as soon as we began to finish some of the training programs, Rick and Laurel started giving us responsibilities in the ministry. The first thing we did was to share our testimony in the big weekly meeting called "College Life," which was usually held in a fraternity or sorority house with perhaps 200 college students in attendance. The first time I did this, I was, to quote Walter Bradley, "scared stiff." But since then, we have shared our testimonies many times on many college campuses. Next, Rick had me teach LTC sessions. We spoke at retreats. I was the main speaker at "College Life." I served for 25 years as faculty advisor to the Campus Crusade for Christ ministry at Alabama. And the list goes on. In fact, when Christian Leadership Ministries first started, one of the Christian Leadership Ministries staff asked Peggy and me to make a list of everything we had done in our involvement with the student ministry to encourage other faculty and staff to get involved. In about 10 minutes of brainstorming, we came up with more than 100 different ways we had been involved. Everything from getting an overhead projector for a meeting to helping Campus Crusade for Christ staff get parking decals to teaching LTC.

Early on, I taught a session of LTC using the book of Nehemiah to highlight "Principles of Leadership." One young man in the class has told me of the impact the course had on his life. He was a young Christian when he took this course about some guy named Nehemiah taught by some guy named Mellichamp. God got Dwayne Craig's attention in a big way. He used the course to give him a clearer sense of purpose and direction. Upon graduation from Alabama, Dwayne joined the staff of Campus Crusade for Christ and ministered on college campuses for several years. He is now a consultant in a large restaurant chain with headquarters here in Atlanta. Every time I see him, he thanks me for the way the Lord used me in his life.

In the Army, they say never volunteer for anything. That's the U.S. Army. In the Lord's army, things are different. If you are looking for a way to reach out to students on your campus and haven't hit on anything yet, go to the director of one of the Christian student ministry groups and volunteer. They might have to check you out a bit at first, but I suspect they will put you to work and provide you with some terrific ministry opportunities.

Hosting International Students

One of the most rewarding ways of ministering to students is to be a host to international students. Many universities and colleges have "Host Family" or "International Friends" programs in which local families and singles serve as hosts to international students. Not in the sense of boarding them in your home as an exchange-type program, but more in terms of being a friend -- someone who cares and who knows how to help as the student (and his or her family) ease into the culture. Have them in your home for an occasional meal and possibly for holidays. We have served for many years as a host family, and Peggy was involved for years as a leader of the host family program at Alabama. Our motivation in this involvement was always to reach out as Christians -- to help internationals understand Christianity and to influence those who were open to Christ. And we have had some rich, rich experiences because of our involvement.

Back in the late 1970s when scholars were just beginning to come to the U.S. from the People's Republic of China, we were the host family to three Chinese scientists -- all a bit older than the usual graduate student. We had them in our home for several meals, and on one occasion, I attempted to engage them in a discussion of spiritual issues. I recall being quite taken aback at their lack of spiritual perception. They confessed that having spent all their lives in an atheistic regime, they had never thought much about spiritual things. As they were preparing to return to China at the end of the year, we had them over for a farewell dinner, and we presented each with a copy of *Evidence That Demands a Verdict* inscribed with my name and academic title, which I reasoned would help them get the books back into their country. I challenged them to read and consider the book. At the end of the evening, as I was driving them back to their apartments, one of them remarked, "I really like Americans, but I like Christians the best." I thought how wonderful that as Christ's ambassadors, we really do stand out in the crowd.

Several years later, the university began an exchange program with several universities in Belgium, and we began to have an influx of Belgian students. Our host family program is probably like most such ventures -- always many more students than hosts. So Peggy and I decided that we would be host family for all the Belgian students. Mind you, we didn't analyze the need and then volunteer to solve the problem -- we just muddled into it. We started with one delightful couple and found out that none of their friends had a host family, so we jumped in to fill what seemed to us to be an unpardonable void. Well, we ended up with six or seven Belgian students, in addition to a few other students from miscellaneous other countries. When we would all get together, the logistics were sometimes pretty awesome. Once we decided to invite all of them to an Easter pageant at one of the local churches and then back to our place for light refreshments. I got to go pick up the Belgian students in my Honda Accord while Peggy went for the others in her Honda Accord. I still laugh thinking of it today. I had one student in the passenger seat in front, one sitting on the gear console with his head sticking through the sun roof, three or four in the back seat, and two in the trunk with the trunk lid open. It was pretty cold in the early spring night air. It's a good thing we didn't have too far to drive or we all might have frozen. Now, you need to get the picture; by then I was a full professor, well-known at the university. And I drove up to the church with nine of us jammed into a five passenger car. Do you think it mattered to them? Not at all. We had a great time together. I expect to this very day they think all Americans are a bit nutty like Dr. Mellichamp.

As I stated earlier, our charge is to help move people to the right in a spiritual sense. Some of our international students have been open to the Gospel and we have seen some of them make decisions for Christ. We have thoroughly enjoyed all of them. And we love them all! We are still in touch with many of them, some in this country and some in their home countries. Many of them are so proud when we visit them to be able to introduce us to their families and friends and associates as their American friends. And how respectful they are of our commitment to Christ. Our Egyptian friends made certain that they took us to see the Coptic museums and historic places, as well as the other Egyptian antiquities when we were in Egypt as their guests. Our Korean friends made sure we had a blessing every time we ate, even in elegant Korean restaurants, and made sure that we saw the Protestant mission churches in Seoul when they hosted our trip there.

Of all the ministry opportunities going, I think the rewards of hosting international students are greatest. My family and I have benefited far more from our relationships with internationals than we have ever given. Yet sadly, many Americans, especially Christians, ignore internationals. Some are even rude or worse to them. Sure, it takes some practice to interact with them. You have to talk a bit slower and you can't use idioms or slang expressions. You have to be patient. We still laugh about the Oriental woman who upon opening a can of Crisco (shortening) was disappointed not to find fried chicken as the picture on the cover plainly showed. But it's all worth it. These people are the influential people in their home countries, the future leaders. What an opportunity for us to have the world in our own back yard. We need to capitalize on the opportunities we have. If you aren't currently reaching out in some ways to internationals, consider doing so.

As I told you, there are many opportunities for us as Christian professors and staff to minister to students -- our own, as well as others. Most of these opportunities are not terribly time intensive. With just a small commitment of time and energy on your part, you can have a significant impact in the lives of students. Remember, all the time I was ministering in the ways I have shared with you, I was heavily involved at the university in research -- publishing, pursuing funding for projects, supervising projects, chairing dissertations -- and had a six-hour teaching load. Part of this time, I was chairman of my department, and part of the time, I was director of the Graduate School of Business. I had family responsibilities as well -- we just involved the family in much of the ministry activity. And I was involved in my church as a college Sunday school teacher for the entire time, as a deacon, and on many committees, too. We somehow manage to find time to do the things that are important to us. Ministering to students is important. We discovered that faithfulness in this sphere of influence can be deeply rewarding

---

5. MINISTERING TO COLLEAGUES

It's one thing to seek to reach out to students; it's quite a different matter to try to reach out in a Christian way to colleagues. Students are here today and gone tomorrow. Some of them are really gone, like to the other side of the world gone. If you botch it in attempting to share with a student, you know that in a little while, the student will be out of the picture. But with colleagues, it's a whole new ball game. They are going to be right next door or down the hall in their office for the next 10, 20, or 30 years. You have to work with them on a daily basis. In some cases, they will be evaluating your work for promotion and tenure. In some cases, you will be doing collaborative work that requires high levels of trust and cooperation with them. If you botch an attempt to minister in the life of a colleague, it could create problems for a long time.

If you are like most Christian professors and staff members, you have felt a burden for your colleagues and have wanted to reach out to them, to minister to them -- especially those closest to you. Perhaps you just haven't done so for fear of turning them off or perhaps it's because you haven't been able to think of an appropriate way to reach out. One of the real keys of ministry with colleagues is to address felt needs. Through the years, we have tried to reach out to colleagues in a number of different ways, all of which seek to focus on a particular need that professors and staff have.

Book Studies

Perhaps the most commonly felt need of professors and staff in academia is time management or personal effectiveness. What better way to minister to busy colleagues who are under pressure to produce than to offer to help them become more effective? Consider leading a weekly discussion of the book, *The Seven Habits of Highly Effective People* by Stephen R. Covey (New York: Simon and Schuster, 1989). This thoughtful book presents seven principles of effectiveness any one of which if followed consistently should enhance effectiveness. The set of seven principles is especially suitable for individuals working in academia; the concepts integrate extremely well in the academic setting. The book can easily be covered in nine or 10 weekly sessions of 45 minutes to an hour. A packet of discussion notes is available from Christian Leadership Ministries, thus, one could lead a discussion group with no additional preparation other than reading the book.

The following steps are suggested for setting up a discussion group.

1. Make a list of several colleagues you wish to include in the group. Six to eight people is probably the most effective group size. Due to conflicts, individuals will miss occasionally; you need a minimum of about six to ensure that on off days you have enough people to have a discussion. With more than eight or so, individuals might feel inhibited and be reluctant to participate. If you are in a large department, you might want to target your group, for example, to assistant professors or to full professors.

2. Begin praying systematically for each person on your list, that God would impress him or her in the area of personal effectiveness and that he or she would respond positively to an invitation to participate in such a group.

3. Make sure that sufficient copies of the book are available from a local bookstore. You might want to consider purchasing copies of the book and giving a gift copy to each person on your list.

4. Challenge each person individually to participate in the study. Obviously, it will be helpful if you have already read the book and started to apply the principles in your own life so that you can use personal illustrations of how the book has helped you. If there are other Christians on your list, you might approach them first and have them pray as you challenge others.

5. Once you have challenged each person on your list, get a schedule of available times either from the individuals or from the department and pick a convenient time for everyone.

Several suggestions will be useful as you begin to meet with the group.

1. Use email or departmental mail to remind each person of the meetings. It only takes about five minutes to send an email message to several people, and it will certainly increase your attendance.

2. Expect from time to time, people will have to miss. It might be possible to juggle the schedule from week to week to maximize attendance, but it is probably best to meet weekly at a regular time, even if a person or two can't make it.

3. Start each session on time and end on time. You could hardly be characterized as effective if you did otherwise and people are more likely to come if they know what to expect in terms of the time requirement.

4. Tell everyone up front that the format is discussion and that everyone is expected to have read the assigned chapter(s) and to participate in the discussion. Be prepared as the leader to ensure that everyone participates; you might have to draw some people into the discussion, and you might have to be careful that some don't monopolize it. Make sure that you don't turn the sessions into a lecture series.

5. Be prepared for some exciting results. Some people will begin to see dramatic changes take place in their marriages and families. Some will

see applications in their instructional duties; some in their research activities. Most will be enthusiastic about having participated; a few might fall by the wayside, mainly for not having read the material or applying the recommendations.

As you conclude the study, several suggestions might be helpful.

1. Think of ways to continue the sessions with a similar focus. A study of *The Man in the Mirror* by Patrick M. Morley (Nashville, TN: Thomas Nelson Publishers, 1992) is an excellent follow-up to the *Seven Habits*. You need to be up front in communicating that while the *Seven Habits* is a secular study, *The Man in the Mirror* is a Christian approach.

2. You might wish to offer the *Seven Habits* to another group, other colleagues, a couple's group, or to a group in your church.

By way of encouragement, let me share my experience at the University of Alabama. When I returned to the University from summer break in 1993, I felt I needed to reach out more to colleagues in my department; to minister, to serve, and to give leadership. I decided to challenge the eight assistant and associate professors in the department to do the *Seven Habits* study. I bit the bullet and purchased eight books and started praying for these eight men.

All eight of them were excited about the study and thought it would be a good thing to do. We met on Friday afternoons from 2 to 2:45 for about 10 Fridays. To summarize the experience, we had a blast! We would talk about applying the principles in the halls and over coffee in the coffee room. Several of us worked to put Covey's scheduling system up on our computers and four or five of us are faithfully using the system to organize our activities. Almost every week, someone in the group would volunteer an application of the material to our work or family situations. Toward the end of our sessions, I suggested that we might like to continue the following semester with *The Man in the Mirror*; six of the eight decided to continue.

When the word got around the department that I was doing the study, two of the full professors came to me and complained, good naturedly, that I had excluded them. I suggested that if the study went well, I would do it again the following semester for the full professors. It went well, so I did it again with four of the five full professors and one of the assistants who had to drop out of the fall study due to an illness in his family. One of the full professors even purchased a copy of the book and started reading it on his own as we were doing the fall study. The department head joined the study for full professors and commended me for exercising this leadership role in the department.

I was so enthusiastic about the study, that the Sunday-evening adult group in our church asked me to lead a study for couples in the church. Some of the people involved in that study have commented on how the study has significantly impacted their lives. I have already had several requests for the discussion notes I prepared from participants who want to start other groups; one such request came from a professor from another university who was visiting the department one Friday afternoon and was invited to the meeting by one of our members.

The bottom line on this whole experience for me is that it has opened the entire faculty up to discussions of effectiveness, cooperation, support, and other topics that foster a collegial atmosphere in a department. My colleague in the next office and I have had frequent and ongoing discussions about how to apply various principles; the study would have been worthwhile just for the way it has helped the two of us. I would encourage you to initiate this activity in your own situation. It is a win/win ministry option -- I can't imagine any down-side risks, and the potential benefits are significant.

As a postscript, since leaving the University of Alabama and moving to Atlanta, I have done two studies here. One was a more conventional study in a research organization setting with much the same outcome as I had in my department This fall, my wife and I decided to use the *Seven Habits* study as a vehicle for reaching out in our neighborhood. We have participated with five couples and three singles working our way through the material. One couple drives 25 miles through Atlanta traffic to attend; another couple drives about 15 miles. We meet every other week (to accommodate my travel schedule) in one of the homes in the neighborhood for about an hour and a half to discuss the material and then have coffee and dessert. We have all thoroughly enjoyed the study, and I think it is safe to say that we have all benefited from it. Some of us have been talking about expanding the group next year into an investigative Bible study for the neighborhood. This is a winner!

Another book study approach that some of us have used to reach out to colleagues is based on the wonderful little book, *How to Be a Christian Without Being Religious* by Fritz Ridenour (Gospel Light Publications, 1967). The book is actually a commentary of Paul's *Letter to the Romans*, but its title and the way in which it was written and illustrated make it ideal for use in an evangelistic book study. The idea that one could be a Christian and *not* be religious has a certain appeal to the unbeliever. The chapter titles are very cleverly done: "Your Faith: Dead or Alive?" "Does God Ever Grade on the Curve?" "Are Christians on Parole or Fully Pardoned?" "Is Your Faith More Than Fire Insurance?" And the illustrations are delightful. There are only 16 short chapters (161 pages) so a study can easily be done in a school term -- semester or quarter -- by doing two chapters per week. There are questions for further thought at the end of each chapter that also facilitate a discussion format. If you have colleagues who might be open to a consideration of spiritual things, you might consider inviting them to your office once a week for eight weeks to discuss the book. Most of the logistical comments given in connection with the *Seven Habits* study apply here as well.

Discussion Series

Search Ministries (address and telephone number available from Christian Leadership Ministries) has developed an effective discussion series approach to reaching out to business and professional people. This approach works well with academics and has been used by a number of professors for reaching out to colleagues. A core of committed Christians is needed to begin with, people who will meet together, preferably in someone's home, one night a week for about four weeks in preparation for the actual outreach. The usual scenario in Christian Leadership Ministries has been to involve four to six couples as hosts. Each couple commits to invite one or more other couples to the outreach phase. The core group meets weekly during the preparation phase to go over the concept with the discussion facilitator, to understand answers to key apologetic questions, to go over some of the actual discussion materials to be used in the outreach phase, and to begin to pray for non-Christian couples they will invite to the outreach phase. The outreach phase lasts two to four weeks and is essentially a free-form discussion series on important topics related to God and life. Questions such as "Why do bad things happen to good people?" and "If man is good, why does he do evil?" are used to start the discussion. The Christians are prepared to participate in the discussion but are careful not to monopolize it.

Several features of this approach account for its effectiveness as an outreach strategy. In the case where the Christians do a good job of recruiting other couples (trusting God to lead them to invite those in whom His Spirit is already at work), the non-believers might outnumber the believers -- possibly by as much as two to one, thus creating a "safe" environment. The believers are committed to maintaining a low-key approach, being neither dogmatic nor authoritative, e.g., "This is what the Bible says, like it or lump it." Thus, the environment is conducive to honest sharing and seeking. The approach focuses on questions participants have about religion or Christianity, thus there is high potential for addressing concerns that might have prevented participants from coming to a saving knowledge of Christ. The discussion time is strictly limited to 59 minutes and 59 seconds and the duration of the series to two to four consecutive weeks. This way, participants know exactly what the time commitment will be up front. An informal time over dessert is usually included after the discussion where people can fellowship and continue to interact over the discussion points.

As you might have guessed, this approach requires a high level of commitment on the part of each of the eight to 12 Christians involved. The time commitment is about two hours for six to eight weekly meetings. The real commitment, however, is inviting colleagues. The couples need to be praying for several weeks about whom they will invite and then muster up the courage to do the actual inviting. It's one thing to talk abstractly about inviting another couple to a discussion series; it's quite another thing to actually invite someone. Of course, if no one does any inviting, no non-Christians will show for the discussion. There also needs to be commitment to follow-up with those who actually participate to the point of actually sharing the Gospel one on one with those who have come to that point through the discussions.

Those who have done this type of outreach are enthusiastic about the experience. It is the kind of thing that would be better if done on a continuing basis, perhaps annually. If you only do one, by the time the host couples have one experience behind them and fully understand the approach, it's over. Although my own experience was limited to one repetition of the series, I suspect that it would have been much more effective had we repeated it again the following year with the same couples involved.

Bible Studies

When individual Christian professors and staff begin to think about having an impact on campus, a Bible study often comes to mind. There are a number of different ways in which a Bible study can be used to minister to colleagues in the university. Let me suggest at least three.

Perhaps the most common situation would be where a number of Christians within the same department or college form a study primarily for fellowship and mutual encouragement. I am aware of many such studies in colleges and universities around the country -- some of these have been in existence for a long time. Usually, such studies begin almost spontaneously when a few people who work in close proximity become aware that they share a common faith and decide to meet on a regular basis. Early in my career, I initiated such a group which included a couple of professors from my "side of the campus" and a couple of graduate students I had met through my involvement in Campus Crusade for Christ. One of the very fruitful studies we undertook was to discover what the Bible had to say about counseling opportunities we might encounter with college students. We also spent a lot of time discussing how we could have a greater impact for Christ in the institution, and it was partly these early discussions that launched me into an exciting career of ministry.

A slightly different twist on this format is where several professors and/or staff members mutually agree to meet together in the context of discipleship. From time to time, I have taken several colleagues aside for a few months of weekly studies. During these sessions, we have studied the Bible topically and also used various Christian books to sharpen our focus. Perhaps the most useful book in this regard is Robert Coleman's *The Master Plan of Evangelism* (Old Tappan, N.J.: Fleming H. Revell Co., 1988), but we have also considered books on time management, marriage, and financial management for the purpose of understanding biblical instruction on a particular topic. I look back on these times and suspect I received as much from them as the men whom I was supposed to be leading through the studies.

Another less-frequently used format is an evangelistic Bible study. Here, the idea is to challenge a number of non-Christian colleagues to meet on a regular basis to discover what the Bible is all about. Obviously, this approach is not for the fainthearted. Walter Bradley has probably followed this model as effectively as anyone I know using *How to Be a Christian Without Being Religious*. I would not recommend trying this without first spending considerable effort in developing prospects for the study. When Walter has used the evangelistic Bible study, it has been after some relationship cultivation and some assessment of interest, usually through a discussion series.

One final way of ministering to colleagues through a Bible study is the couple's Bible study. For many years in Tuscaloosa, I led a Bible study for couples that involved mainly university employees and their spouses, but also included several couples who were not connected at all with the university. We had a pretty stable core of Christian couples who were very committed to each other and to the group as well. Most of these people were outreach-oriented, so every year, they would invite friends and acquaintances to join the group. Peggy and I saw the group as a natural place to invite our non-Christian university colleagues -- the fellowship was warm and the environment was open toward seekers. We met each week in a different home for about an hour of study followed by dessert and fellowship. Some close relationships were formed -- we attended conferences together and some of us vacationed together. Through the years, we saw a number of people come to Christ either through the group directly or as a consequence of the group including a department chairman, several married doctoral students, and children of the couples involved in the study. One time, I was voicing some regrets that I was not as effective as I wanted to be in impacting people for Christ when Tommy Howard, one of the faithful members of the couple's Bible study, gently replied that he was offended by my remarks; he said the Bible study had had an enormous impact on his own life and the life of everyone in his family.

I am also big on activities that simultaneously accomplish more than one objective. The couple's Bible study is a wonderful way of involving your spouse in ministry while cultivating deep relationships with other Christian couples. Recently, we received an email message from a couple involved in our couple's Bible study years ago. We had almost lost touch with them because they moved from Tuscaloosa 20 years ago and we moved two years ago. We are planning a get together again soon. We are really looking forward to seeing them as they have been our soul-mates in ministry over the years, even though we haven't been in close touch.

It should be pretty clear that all of the formats described here for ministering to colleagues through Bible studies require a fairly serious time commitment. We are talking about a weekly meeting with some outside preparation for anywhere from a few weeks as in the case of an evangelistic study, to several years for a couple's study. However, the benefits of such studies in terms of transformed lives always outweigh any expenditure of time and energy we might make. If you are at all gifted in the area of teaching and this seems like a good ministry fit for you, I would encourage you to do it.

I want to register one small word of caution at this point regarding faculty/staff Bible studies. A Bible study is **not** the appropriate vehicle for fundamentally impacting the university for Christ. This purpose is effectively accomplished through the Christian Faculty/Staff Fellowship, which is discussed in the next section. Unfortunately, professors and staff often get involved in a Bible study that they view as the "be all, end all," and they use the study as an excuse not to get involved in more comprehensive efforts to impact the campus. More on this later.

Mentoring

I think mentoring junior colleagues is a perfect ministry opportunity for Christian professors and I would like to see us really begin to capitalize on this. I have mentioned before that effective ministry should be needs-based -- we have to become more aware of the needs of those to whom we are seeking to minister. One need that every new professor in the university has is in the area of professional development. The business world has long recognized the value of mentoring. Talk to any executive in a large business organization, and he will quickly let you know that having a mentor is an imperative for personal success in business. Most successful professors in the university, likewise, can point to a senior professor who has had an impact on them personally. Unfortunately in the university, we have not been nearly as intentional in this respect as our counterparts in business.

Those in the university who are senior professors and well-established in their careers need to see mentoring younger professors as a significant ministry possibility. Consider coming alongside one or two young professors in your discipline and helping them to succeed in the academy -- help them get their research programs off to a good start and help them become effective classroom teachers. If the person you are mentoring is not a Christian, you will have many natural opportunities for talking to him about spiritual matters, perhaps by sharing with him your personal goals and objectives, which would, of course, include spiritual goals. If the individual is a Christian, you will have opportunities to encourage him toward spiritual maturity. We aren't talking about a great time commitment here -- perhaps an hour or so a month. The payoff could be considerable.

One of the ministry opportunities we will discuss in the next section is the Tenure Seminar. As you and your Christian colleagues reach out in this way to junior colleagues in the institution, you might have good opportunities to establish mentoring relationships with junior faculty colleagues in other departments. And in Christian Leadership, we ultimately want to put in place a mechanism for mentoring on a national and international basis, putting young professors in touch with Christian scholars (without respect to geographic location) in their disciplines who can help them succeed. This is probably a few years in the future; for the present we need to develop a mindset that views mentoring as a fruitful ministry opportunity.

6. FOCUSED RESEARCH/TEACHING

Most of us who teach and do research in the university do so in disciplines that are relatively sterile with respect to spiritual content. Only a very few of us teach in disciplines where spiritual issues arise frequently and naturally in the content of the subject as, for example, in philosophy or history. Likewise, only a few of us would be able to write and publish pieces that have any appreciable spiritual content. Not many of us have the opportunity to publish a work like Phillip Johnson's *Reason in the Balance* (Downers Grove, IL: Inter-Varsity Press, 1995) in the course of our normal research inquiries. The words *naturally* and *normal* are significant here. In the normal course of our inquiries and in the natural pursuit of our teaching, we might not have opportunities to address spiritual concerns. But we need to be much more intentional in our teaching and research than we are. We need to seek appropriate venues in teaching and research for engaging in a Christian way in this regard. Several possibilities exist.

Specialized Courses

Often, with a bit of creativity, we can find an area within our discipline that is more amenable to spiritual issues than the area we usually target. The area of ethics immediately comes to mind although there are many other examples. Ethics just happens to be a current "hot button" in most academic disciplines these days. Many academic departments and, indeed, colleges are attempting to increase the coverage of ethics in individual courses and in programs. Many accrediting agencies are pushing for increased coverage of ethical issues in programs. Philosophy of science is another area where there is pressure to develop specialized course offerings. These trends offer many of us a unique opportunity to develop courses to meet the demands. As Christians, we are often uniquely qualified to develop and present such offerings to students. There doesn't have to be a strong component of Christian content in such courses; remember, it only takes a slight opening for you to communicate to students where you stand with regard to matters of faith.

Secular Publications

In the same way, there are opportunities to address spiritual issues in our research areas if we will just look with an open mind. Again, in the area of ethics, many journals in business, engineering, medicine, and law are open to articles that explore ethical considerations. Bill Jordan, Professor of Mechanical Engineering at Louisiana Tech, made a decision to "tithe" his research in this context several years ago. He decided to target approximately 10 percent of his research effort to issues within the field of engineering ethics. As a result, he regularly publishes his findings in mainline engineering journals. What an effective approach. This is another of those double-duty ideas that allows us to accomplish several objectives at one time. Bill is simultaneously getting good publications in good journals in his field and using the ethical focus as a platform for a variety of ministry openings with students and associates as well. What about your discipline? Are there similar opportunities? Have you ever considered tithing your research?

Christian Publications

Many of us work in disciplines or at least have interests in areas that qualify us to write for Christian media. For some, these opportunities will "count" from an academic perspective, e.g., articles in archaeology or history in a scholarly Christian journal; for others there may be no direct academic spin-off such as in the case of the book chapter on "Applying Biblical Principles in Operations Research and Information Systems" that I wrote for a Christian book. However, as I mentioned in the paragraph on "Issues Papers," I realized significant indirect benefits from this exercise. If you have an interest along these lines, I urge you to begin to develop it for publication in appropriate Christian media. This is important if we are to win the battle of ideas.

I hope that as you have read through this section on "Ministering Individually" you have been impressed with the many ministry options we have as individual Christian professors and staff in the secular university. I know many of you have discovered other effective ways of reaching out to students and colleagues and I hope that you will let me hear about them so that we might incorporate them in future versions. If you are not currently reaching out to those around you in the university, I would encourage you to begin now. Select one of the approaches outlined that seems to fit your temperament and circumstances and begin to implement it. If you have questions about a particular approach after reading the material here, contact our Christian Leadership Ministries headquarters in Dallas; they will be happy to respond to your questions. As you begin to reach out, ask God to honor your efforts and then step out in faith.

Remember, I also pointed out that there are a number of ministry activities that you should be addressing in your position as a Christian professor or staff member of a university or college. Perhaps we should briefly review the "required" things. Every Christian professor and staff member should have prepared his personal testimony; this includes having a written, polished version, as well as being prepared to orally share it in appropriate situations. Every Christian professor and researcher should have thought through his discipline from a Christian perspective and have developed a position paper or talk that details the salient points. Every Christian professor ought to find an effective way to communicate that he is a Christian to his students. Every Christian professor or staff member who teaches freshmen and/or sophomores should be helping them succeed academically through "How to Make Better Grades" or "Time Management" talks. We need to ensure that our office decorations are communicating an appropriate message. We should be reaching out to international students and professors in friendship. And we need to be more intentional in terms of seeing our teaching and research as potential means for communicating a Christian witness. Wow! That's a lot of homework. Don't wait until you've finished all the required stuff before striking out on the optional approaches -- if you do, you may never get to the really fun ministry opportunities.

PART TWO:

MINISTERING WITH OTHERS ON CAMPUS

In the summer of 1970, Peggy and I attended a conference for Christian professors and staff at Arrowhead Springs, California. It was during this conference that I was challenged by Jim Engel, Walter Bradley and others for the first time to begin to think about how I could use my position as a Christian professor as a platform to have an impact for Christ on my campus and to reach out to students and colleagues. As I returned to the campus that fall, I started to reach out in small ways as an individual, using some of the approaches described in the previous section. But my background in industrial engineering convinced me that if I wanted to have the maximum impact possible, I would need to work cooperatively with other like-minded faculty and staff on the campus. In fact, the principle of synergy was so well ingrained in my thinking, I never even considered not working with others. The only questions I had were where? how?

Sometime during this timeframe, I met a young Christian professor in the Music Department named Paul Headwall, and we started meeting together weekly for lunch to pray for the campus and to talk about what we could do to have an impact for Christ. Shortly after Paul and I started meeting together, we were joined by Dave Masoner, a young professor in the College of Education. As we talked and strategized, it became obvious that we needed a leader, a point man; we needed someone visible as a Christian in the community and preferably a full professor. We were all new assistant professors. We floated our ideas by two men who met all of our criteria and that is exactly what happened -- the ideas floated right by them over their heads. It was clear to me that if we were going to initiate something among the Christian faculty and staff at the University of Alabama, I was going to have to be the person to get things going. So around 1972, I determined we were going to have a faculty/staff fellowship at the university if it was a fellowship of one -- me. I didn't know exactly what form it would take; I didn't know what we would do. I just knew we needed to be meeting together to pray, to encourage, and to discuss what we could do to make a difference.

It would have been terrific if we could have picked up the phone and called Christian Leadership Ministries and had them send out someone to tell us what to do and how to do it. Unfortunately, Christian Leadership Ministries did not exist at the time. So Paul, Dave, and I started meeting together on a regular basis. At first it was the three of us; then four; then six. We talked, we prayed, and through the years since then we have learned by experimentation. I wish I could say that we thought everything out in advance and then it was simply a matter of implementation. That is not what happened. We learned by trial and error. Things that worked, we remembered and continued to do. Things that didn't work, we tried to forget and not repeat. Gradually over the years, we came up with some of the ideas and models I will be sharing with you in this section.

During this same timeframe, Walter Bradley was attempting to do much the same thing on his campuses, first at the Colorado School of Mines and later at Texas A&M University. In 1972, Peggy and I affiliated formally with Campus Crusade for Christ as associate staff members, and we saw Walter and Ann off and on through the years. Whenever we would get together, we would compare notes and return to our campuses determined to ramp things up to the next level. When Campus Crusade for Christ formed Christian Leadership Ministries in 1980, Walter and I were asked to speak at the first conferences the new ministry would host for faculty and university staff. Our first seminar was in Atlanta at an airport motel; we spent about 15 minutes planning for three hours of seminar time for the 70-80 people who were registered for the conference. In that first series of talks, we switched telling war stories about how we had tried to reach students and colleagues and things we had done with other university people to try to impact our campuses. It was all we knew at the time. Through the years, we have been joined by many others, and we have tried to be a bit more intentional and smarter at what we are doing, nevertheless; many of the ideas in this manual date back to those early days.

I have always viewed the Christian Faculty/Staff Fellowship as the crucial element in ministering together with others on campus. Everything else we do on campus that relates to corporate ministry flows naturally out of the fellowship. In this section, I want to describe the entire spectrum of faculty/staff ministry on a university campus. We'll start with a detailed description of what the fellowship is and how to organize and sustain one. Then we'll look at a number of activities that arise from the fellowship. Obviously your first task if you are considering initiating joint faculty/staff ministry on your campus is to establish a Christian Faculty/Staff Fellowship. I have not always known exactly how to do the fellowship, at least not in a way that was transferable. It has only been since leaving the University of Alabama and being able to objectively assess what we were doing there that I have been able to articulate the plan in a way that is transferable. Here is how you might go about starting things on your campus.

7. THE CHRISTIAN FACULTY/STAFF FELLOWSHIP

The Christian university professor or staff member who is serious about having an influence for Christ at his or her institution will quickly realize that to achieve the maximum influence, one must work together with other like-minded Christians on campus. This is the principle of synergy at work -- the simultaneous action of separate agencies that, together, have greater total effect than the sum of their individual effects. The author of the Letter to the Hebrews underscores this point by writing, "And let us consider how to stimulate one another to love and good deeds, not forsaking our own assembling together as is the habit of some but encouraging one another; and all the more as you see the day drawing nearer" (Hebrews 10:24,25). That the principle is true hardly requires debate; the question is how does one go about initiating cooperative relationships with other Christian professors and staff in the midst of the demands and pressures of daily institutional activity? The answer is the Christian Faculty/Staff Fellowship, which is described in this section.

Purpose

What is a Christian Faculty/Staff Fellowship? I like to think of the fellowship in terms of a *think tank* or *research and development activity* through which faculty and staff come together on a regular basis to creatively think about, discuss, and plan how they as Christians can individually and corporately impact students, colleagues and the institution for the cause of Christ. Professors are among the most creative individuals in our society. Unfortunately, most professors focus a significant part of their creativity on their academic discipline. If just a fraction of this combined creativity can be focused on the issue of impacting the university for Christ, much will happen. In addition to this creative function, the fellowship should be the umbrella under which all corporate faculty ministry activity occurs; it should be the initiator and sponsor of corporate faculty ministry on the campus.

What is meant by "regular?" Weekly. Anything less than weekly will not be adequate to develop the level of commitment and depth of relationships that will be necessary to profoundly impact the institution for Christ. Many protest saying, "This is a good idea, but couldn't we meet monthly or twice a month?" My response is why would you not want to meet weekly? The only legitimate reason one can offer is that the activity just isn't a high enough priority. For a Christian professor or staff member, this should be a top priority. Each of us will ultimately be required to give an account of our lives and our ministries. I believe that one day I will stand before the Lord and give an account of my life. I believe that He will be considerably more interested in what I did on my campus to influence people for the Savior than in how many refereed journals articles I published. I just don't think that protesting to the Lord that my research commitments and teaching loads prevented me from participating with colleagues in impacting the university for Christ will wash. So the fellowship should meet weekly.

Broadly speaking, the fellowship should accomplish two purposes. First, it is to be the means by which professors and staff determine how to impact students, colleagues, and the institution for Christ and through which they cooperatively work to accomplish this end. Secondly, the fellowship should minister to the faculty and staff who constitute its membership. In this context, the fellowship should promote and foster deep relationships between and among its members. It should impart vision to its members and equip them for the work of ministry. It should help members to pursue excellence in their work within the institution and within the larger community. And it should support and uplift members when they experience difficult times.

Now, before we discuss how the fellowship accomplishes these important purposes, let me offer a word of caution by stating what the fellowship is not. The fellowship is *not* a faculty and/or staff Bible study! It's interesting, when Christian faculty and staff get together and begin to think about having an impact for Christ in the university, often the first thing that comes to mind is a Bible study. We are not talking about a Bible study. This is an important element of the Christian life, but it is not to be the only or *primary* pursuit of the fellowship. I am aware of *no* faculty or staff Bible study that has had a significant impact on a university or college, even though some have been existence for decades. I am aware of many instances in which faculty/staff Bible studies have started and slowly faded away. The focus of a Bible study simply is not global or outward enough. The fellowship must focus on the issue of impacting the institution for Christ and equipping its members to accomplish this task.

Furthermore, the fellowship is not to be a substitute for the local church. People have told me regarding the fellowship, "I don't want to do anything in our fellowship that I can do in my church!" The fellowship should confine its focus to helping its members to (1) become better professors or staff members or (2) become better *Christian* professors or staff members. If the fellowship confines its focus to these issues, it becomes "the only game in town," that is, the only place I can go to help me succeed as a Christian academic in the university. Thus, if I am at all serious about wanting to be a better professor or staff member or if I want to have an effective influence for Christ in my workplace, I will see the fellowship as necessary in accomplishing these aims and will be committed to it.

Structure

A schematic diagram of the faculty/staff ministry in a university or college is shown in Figure 7-1. The focal point of activity for any faculty ministry should be the weekly fellowship. The major goal of the fellowship, as we have discussed, is to impact students, faculty, staff, and the institution for Christ. A necessary secondary goal is to engage faculty and staff in the fellowship. This is done in a number of ways as shown in Figure 7-1. The most obvious way is to identify Christians among the faculty and staff and challenge them to become a part of the fellowship. Persistence is a virtue here. I am aware of one individual, a very committed Christian, who observed our group with detached interest for five or six years before ever seeing the benefit or value of joining with us. Another way to engage individuals in the fellowship is to reach them through various "filter" events that communicate a Christian message to the faculty and staff of the institution at large, i.e., various outreach activities. Thus, the general idea shown in Figure 7-1 is to move individuals from the population of *All Faculty/Staff* to the population of *Christian Faculty/Staff* to the population of *Weekly Fellowship*.

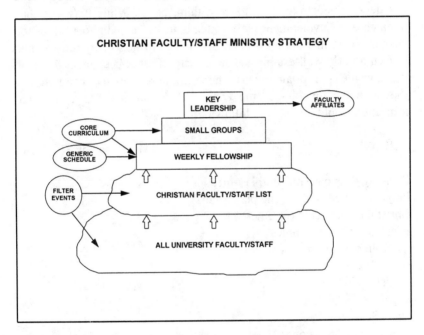

Figure 7-1. Schematic Diagram of the Christian Faculty/Staff Ministry.

Notice from the diagram that *Small Groups* are a part of the faculty ministry. These will normally be *ad hoc* groups set up for a variety of purposes that will be identified and described later. Obviously, to undertake such a ministry in an institution of higher learning, there must be a core of leadership committed to the philosophy of impacting the institution for Christ; this core is shown in the diagram as *Key Leadership* and may be an actual group that meets to oversee the ministry. Or it may simply be the collection of individuals who give leadership to the ministry. One or more of the key leaders may chose to formally affiliate with Christian Leadership Ministries as a *Faculty Affiliate*. More on the advisability of having an actual planning or steering committee later.

Activities

Recall that the fellowship is intended to function in a research and development role; it is to be a think tank. While it is true that research and development activity tends to be serendipitous, it is not recommended that the fellowship be allowed to float willy-nilly along. In fact, a fairly well-established set of activities has been identified that will give the appropriate focus to the fellowship. This set of activities is shown in the diagram as the *Generic Schedule* and for a semester institution would include the following:

Activity	Meetings per Semester
Planning Sessions (first and last meeting)	2
Prayer and Fellowship (one per month)	3
Christian Leadership (or other) Training	2
Faculty/Staff Testimonies	2
Discipline Position Papers	2
Book Review	1
Ministry Update	1
Legal Issues Update	1
Open Session	1
Total Sessions	15

It should be emphasized at this point that these will not necessarily be the only activities of the fellowship, nor are the recommended number of sessions hard and fast requirements. This is a good basic mix of activities that will interest Christian professors and staff and that are fairly easy to put together into a semester program. In fact, I would suggest that a mix of activities is superior to concentrating on any one thing for very long for a practical reason. Suppose, for example, you decide to schedule a six-session sequence on creation/evolution (this happens to be a popular subject for most faculty and staff). If I happen not to be interested in this topic and I'm not absolutely committed to the group, I'll just drop out for a while and stop coming. Once that happens, it will be difficult if not impossible for you to get me back in the group. It should also be obvious from these suggestions that the agenda is not to be a Bible study.

Each of the activities in the *Generic Schedule* will now be described in a bit more detail.

Planning Sessions. (Two Meetings Per Semester.) Now let's address the issue of whether to have a planning or steering committee. Often, when faculty initiate an activity or program of some magnitude, such as a faculty ministry, a steering committee is proposed to oversee things. I would advise against this approach for two reasons, both learned from actual experience. First, a steering committee requires time; it has meetings. You will be asking every member of the steering committee for several hours of time each semester -- if you can accomplish the planning function without this investment, you're way ahead. Furthermore, when working with busy people, it is usually difficult to find a time when they can all meet. Second, when a steering committee comes up with a program for an organization, any organization, it is the steering committee's plan; it's difficult to engender ownership by the rank-and-file membership of the group.

Both of these important objections can easily be overcome by doing the planning activity within the context of the entire group -- the entire fellowship. By devoting two weekly meetings a semester to the planning function, you obviate the need for a steering committee and the program that emerges is everyone's program -- you don't have to sell it to the group. Now this might not be quite as effective as a planning committee, especially at first, but I can assure you based on 20 plus years of experience, it works, and it works extremely well. However, if you insist on having a steering committee, go ahead -- just know that you are adding a significant overhead burden to your activity.

First Meeting. Attend to basic organizational details; i.e., mission statement; meeting dates, location and times and introduction of members. Allow most of the time for members to suggest topics for future meetings and volunteer to be coordinators (invite speaker, prepare book review, prepare position paper, etc.). The goal for this planning time is to generate a list of potential topics for the following semester and to fill any holes in the schedule for the present semester.

Last Meeting. Firm up the schedule for the following semester; i.e., the last meeting in the fall is when you set the schedule of topics for the spring.

Remember, when selecting topics one, or both of the following criteria should be met:

1. Topics will help members become better professors or staff.
2. Topics will help members become better Christian professors or staff.

Prayer and Fellowship. (One Meeting Per Month.) One meeting each month should be devoted to building relationships among the members of the fellowship and praying for the university administration, campus concerns and requests of members. To accomplish these objectives, it is suggested that members introduce themselves to the group and briefly share pertinent personal information. Some light discussion on topics of general interest can also be used to build relationships. A prayer list should be developed and maintained for the group, and it should be used to guide the prayer time. As you probably know, many prayer times devote most of the allotted time to sharing prayer requests with very little time actually spent praying.

Training. (Two Sessions per Semester.) At least two sessions per semester should be devoted to equipping members of the fellowship in ministry and/or professional skills. Ministry skills include testimony preparation, learning to share one's faith, how to have an effective devotional life and prayer life, etc. Professional skills include time and life management principles, teaching effectiveness skills, research skills, etc. Christian Leadership Ministries is in the process of putting together a *Core Curriculum* that defines a spectrum of capabilities one should acquire as one grows toward Christian maturity. The Core Curriculum is shown in Figure 7-1 as an input to both the *Weekly Fellowship* and to *Small Groups*, for example, a discipleship group.

Faculty/Staff Testimonies. (Two Per Semester.) Every Christian professor and staff member needs to be equipped to share his personal testimony in a formal situation, i.e., classroom or meeting environment.

An effective way to ensure that the members of the fellowship are thus equipped is to periodically have a member share his testimony with the fellowship.

Position Papers. (Two Per Semester.) Every Christian professor needs to have thought through his academic discipline to determine how the Christian worldview impacts the discipline or to identify the tension points between the discipline and Christianity. This thought process then needs to be formally developed as a *white paper* or position paper. Each semester, professors who have been engaged in this process should be encouraged to present the results of their assessment to the fellowship for consideration and feedback.

Book Review. (One Per Semester.) Many Christian professors and staff are not well informed of the battle being waged in the university today. I routinely ask how many participants in my seminars have read some of the key books that should be required reading for Christian professors; the vast majority have not. Having a member of the fellowship review a relevant book each semester is a good way to challenge members to begin to read some of the important works. A few suggested titles are:

1. *A Christian Critique of the University.* Charles Habib Malik, Downers Grove, IL: Inter-Varsity Press, 1982.
2. *The Soul of the American University.* George M. Marsden, New York: Oxford University Press, 1994.
3. *The Closing of the American Mind.* Allan Bloom, New York: Simon and Schuster, 1987.
4. *Impostors in the Temple.* Martin Anderson, New York: Simon and Schuster, 1992.
5. *Reason in the Balance.* Phillip Johnson, Downers Grove, IL: Inter-Varsity Press, 1995.

Christian Student Ministry Update. (One Per Semester.) Many faculty members are not informed about what Christian students are up to and up against in the institution. It is pretty difficult to know how to impact students for the Savior if you don't know what they are experiencing spiritually in the environment. One of the best ways to become informed in this context is to have the directors and student leaders of the various evangelical student ministries come to brief the fellowship periodically on their activities. Students are usually so enthusiastic about their endeavors that their enthusiasm spills over and infects the fellowship members. Having students share about a summer mission project or an evangelistic meeting in a fraternity or sorority can be challenging to members who might never think about getting out of their comfort zone. The number of evangelical student groups varies from campus to campus -- one large Midwestern campus has 55 such organizations.

Legal Issues Update. (One Per Year.) Christian professors and staff need to understand the responsibilities and prerogatives of academic freedom as guaranteed by the U.S. Constitution. Many professors and staff do not understand these issues, and as a result, many Christian academics do nothing for fear of offending. An effective way of equipping fellowship members in this arena is to have a First Amendment lawyer periodically discuss constitutional rights of academics and to summarize national/regional/local cases. Christian Leadership Ministries also has an excellent video workshop in the legal issues area that is available through its Dallas headquarters.

Pastor's Briefing. (Once Every Other Year.) Pastors are usually uninformed as to what it's like to be a Christian professor or staff member in a secular university or college. As a result, they frequently encourage academics in their congregation to minister almost exclusively within the church and fail to realize that for the Christian academic, the campus should be a primary place of ministry. The Pastor's Briefing is a wonderful venue for addressing this problem. Each member of the fellowship invites his pastor to the weekly meeting. The program for that week relates what it is like to be a Christian professor or staff member in the secular university -- the pressures and the opportunities.

Open Session. (One per Semester.) An open session each semester (usually midway into the semester) needs to be left in the schedule to allow flexibility to respond to various opportunities. From time to time things will happen on campus that require a response from the fellowship and necessitate discussion and deliberation. Occasionally, one or more members will suggest that the fellowship explore a particular opportunity, for example, an evangelistic outreach event, and the group will need time to discuss and plan appropriate actions.

The prospect of putting together a weekly program for a 15-week semester computes to a lot of work in the minds of most faculty members. However, as the blank schedule in Exhibit 7-1 shows, when you use two sessions for planning and three sessions for prayer and fellowship, there are only 10 slots left to be filled. A couple of training activities, a couple of testimonies, a couple of position papers, a book review, a ministry update, and an open session, and the schedule is booked. An example of a semester schedule that follows this scheme is also included in Exhibit 7-1.

Getting Organized

Most universities don't have a formal process for faculty and staff to follow to obtain official university recognition -- it's like if you decide to be an official university group, you are. Even so, it is probably a good idea to check with the people (usually in the Office of Student Affairs) who supervise the process for student organizations. They might ask you to fill out some paperwork and might request something on the order of a statement of purpose. A copy of our statement of purpose from the University of Alabama along with our statement of faith is included as Exhibit 7-2 -- you may use these materials or modify them as desired for your organization.

One word of caution at this point. On very rare occasions, overzealous administrative minions have attempted to make things difficult for faculty/staff groups attempting to get organized. In general, there is very clear legal precedent for Christian groups to have the same access to university and college facilities as non-religious groups. This includes access to meeting rooms (subject to availability, of course), campus mail, electronic mail, and the campus telephone system. If your institution accords access to these facilities to *any* student or faculty group, it must grant the same access to *all* groups. If by the remotest of circumstances you should encounter such opposition, a courteous, but firm letter to the person's superior with perhaps a copy to the University Legal Counsel should ensure smooth sailing.

Exhibit 7-1.   Semester Calendars Utilizing the Generic Fellowship
                Model.

ANYWHERE UNIVERSITY
Christian Faculty/Staff Fellowship
Spring 1998 Schedule

Date		Topic	Coordinator
January	14	Introduction, Planning	
	21		
	28		
February	4	Prayer & Fellowship	
	11		
	18		
	25		
March	4	Spring Break	
	11	Prayer & Fellowship	
	18		
	26		
April	1	Prayer & Fellowship	
	8		
	15		
	22		
	29	Plan for Fall	

Exhibit 7-1. Continued.

PURDUE UNIVERSITY
Christian Faculty/Staff Fellowship
Spring 1996 Schedule

Date		Topic	Coordinator
January	17	Introduction, Planning	Jim Jones
	24	Racial Reconciliation	Mike Bartel
	31	Fellowship and Prayer	
February	7	Personal Testimony	Bob Chalmers
	14	Christian Attitudes in Research and Teaching	Steve Schneider
	21	The New Age Movement in Nursing	Joan Kuipers
	28	Fellowship and Prayer	
March	6	Spring Break	
	13	Ministering to Chinese Students	Keith Spence
	20	Internet Resources for Christians	Scott King
	27	Fellowship and Prayer	
April	3	International Students and Scholars	Mike Brzezinski
	10	Short Term International Opportunities	Rich Grant
	17	Creation Evolution Issues	Cliff Johnston
	24	Fellowship and Prayer	
May	1	Open	
	8	Plan for Fall	Jim Dunn

Exhibit 7-2. Example Statement of Purpose and Statement of Belief.

UNIVERSITY OF ALABAMA
CHRISTIAN FACULTY/STAFF FELLOWSHIP
Statement of Purpose

Recognizing the great influence we have by virtue of our positions on the faculty and staff of the University of Alabama and desiring to use our influence to impact the university community and, indeed, higher education for the Lord Jesus Christ, we affirm our obedience to His command in Acts 1:8, ". . . and you shall be My witnesses . . ."

"In Jerusalem," -- On the University of Alabama Campus

By maintaining a Christian Faculty/Staff Fellowship on the campus for the purpose of:

1. Developing and implementing a comprehensive strategy for cultivating our individual relationships with the Lord and effecting a unified impact on the campus.

2. Sharing of mutual concerns and interests with colleagues through discussion and prayer.

3. Providing a forum for communicating information regarding various Christian activities on campus.

4. Providing opportunities for various types of Christian training.

5. Serving as a resource for Christian campus and community organizations to provide speakers, endorsement for activities and programs, etc.

"In Judea and Samaria," -- Regionally, Nationally

By investigating and promoting opportunities for involvement with other Christian faculty and staff on a regional and national level.

By identifying Christian colleagues on other campuses and encouraging them to become involved in similar efforts.

By developing an awareness of issues facing higher education and society and by determining effective responses to these issues from the Christian community.

"To the Remotest Part of the Earth." -- Worldwide

By developing strategies for multiplying our ministries as we, our students and our associates go to the world.

Exhibit 7-2. Continued.

UNIVERSITY OF ALABAMA
CHRISTIAN FACULTY/STAFF FELLOWSHIP

Statement of Belief

A. We accept the authority of the Word of God as the only infallible rule of faith and life. 2 Timothy 3:16; 2 Peter 1:21; John 10:35

B. We believe in one eternal and triune God. This God is Creator and Lord of the world governing all things according to the purpose of His will. Matthew 28:19; Isaiah 40:28; Ephesians 1:11

C. We believe in only one Savior, the Lord Jesus Christ. 1 Timothy 2:5,6; Galatians 1:6-9; John 3:16; Acts 4:12

D. We believe the Father sent the Holy Spirit to bear witness to the Son. Conviction of sin, faith in Jesus, new birth and Christian growth are all the Spirit's work. John 15:26,27; 16:8-11; 1 Corinthians 12:3; Acts 1:8; Galatians 5:22,23

E. We believe that God created man as male and female and that they were created in His image. We also believe that man fell into sin, yet he still bears God's image. The present natural state of man is dead in sins and trespasses. Genesis 1:27; 3:1-14; Romans 5:12; Ephesians 2:3; 4:18

F. We believe in the necessity of conversion -- not of a particular conversion experience, for experiences vary -- but of convertedness, in the sense of a quality of life that shows signs of repentance and faith and, thus, new birth. Titus 3:4-7; John 3:4-8; Acts 2:37-39; 2 Timothy 2:25,26

G. We believe that God is both Creator and Judge of all men and nations. We therefore should share His love and concern for the world and it's people. We believe that evangelism and citizenship are both part of our Christian responsibility. The salvation we claim should transform the totality of our personal and social responsibilities. Acts 17:24-31; Matthew 5:14-16; Amos 5:21-24; Micah 6:8; James 2:14-26

From an organizational standpoint, very little is needed in terms of officers, job descriptions, etc. A fellowship can function effectively with only a few dignitaries. You will need a leader or director; this will be the person who keeps everything going. Thus, he or she should be absolutely committed to the fellowship and see it as a very high priority. The leader is ultimately responsible for the weekly program, although by farming out responsibility for individual meetings to interested members, this turns out not to be a very difficult task. I directed our group at the University of Alabama for 20 plus years and rarely spent more than about 30 minutes a week keeping things on track. You will need someone, preferably with some financial skills, to keep track of the fellowship's money. As we will see, most of the special events that the fellowship undertakes require financing; it is not uncommon for a fellowship to have an annual budget amounting to several thousand dollars per year. You also need someone to be responsible for communication with members each week, i.e., reminding them of the meeting. Good computer skills are helpful here. And finally, you will need someone to oversee student newspaper ads that will normally be done on a semester or yearly basis. If these four or five people will commit a few minutes a week on a consistent basis to attend to their duties, the fellowship should run smoothly.

Meeting Mechanics

The meeting time and place for the fellowship are important considerations. Most successful fellowships that I am aware of meet during the lunch hour. Most professors and staff members take a break for lunch, so the habit of spending the lunch hour with colleagues is attractive as a way of accomplishing two purposes at once. I would suggest that you pick a day of the week when most of your people are available and stick with that day on a permanent basis. If your people always know that the fellowship meets on a certain day, say Wednesday, they will begin to block that time out automatically and commit to the meeting even as one would a civic group or other group that meets on a specific day. I am aware of groups that have tried to shift the day around from semester to semester to accommodate most of the members -- I am convinced that all this accomplishes is to foster a lower level of commitment from the members. What we want to happen is for the members, over time, to accommodate their schedules to the fellowship. Several years ago, one of our members called me the first week of the semester, and in a bit of a dither he explained that his department chairman had scheduled him for class at noon on Wednesdays that semester. "Could we change the fellowship this semester to Thursday at noon?" My response was, "I'm really sorry, but the fellowship meets on Wednesdays; it has always met on Wednesdays and will continue to meet on Wednesdays." We lost him for the semester, but he spoke to his chairman and rearranged his schedule to have Wednesday noon open.

For a noon meeting, a centrally located meeting place preferably with dining facilities is needed. Many fellowships meet in the University Center or Student Union so members can pick up something to eat on the way into the meeting or pick up a drink for a brown bag lunch from home. If you can get the same room semester after semester, it will help the consistency of your group. It helps in this regard to know the person who makes room assignments; our fellowship has met in the same room for many years, thanks to a staff person who is supportive of what we are trying to do. We send her a thank-you note from time to time to express appreciation for her help.

For large, geographically dispersed campuses, finding a convenient location might be virtually impossible, and even if one is available, parking can be a problem. In such cases, having smaller fellowships in more than one location might be indicated. I am very reluctant to advocate multiple fellowships. On most campuses, it is a real challenge to get past the critical mass of people necessary for a vibrant group; multiple groups only exacerbate this difficulty. I would go along with a separate group perhaps for medical centers/schools where the environment is very different from the average university or college campus, but, in general, I recommend one fellowship per campus.

If you elect to meet at noon, you might try scheduling your program to occur from 12:15 to 12:50. This way people know they can get through a serving line or arrive a bit late from an 11 o'clock class without missing any of the program, and those who have 1 o'clock engagements can slip out a bit early without missing much other than possibly some Q&A at the end of the meeting. The time from noon to 12:15 turns out to be a good time of fellowship and informal interaction, as does the time at the end of the hour; several people usually hang around past 1 o'clock to interact on various issues.

Since professors and staff members are busy people, you will need some kind of reminder system. Campus mail is effective in this regard, but can be time-consuming if weekly announcements are sent to every member of the group. Electronic mail is an easy way of communicating with members to remind them of the meeting time and place, as well as the specific program offering for the week. As many of us do our weekly planning either on Friday afternoon or Monday morning, a Friday noon announcement probably is the most effective. Unfortunately, many faculty members stay chronically behind with email or they delete messages without reading them. Thus, the most effective way of staying in touch with the group is probably with telephone reminders. For a number of years, we hired an undergraduate student to make weekly calls -- for a very modest financial investment, you get the reminders out and help a needy student at the same time. The best option is probably a combination of email and phone calls.

As a final comment under the heading of meeting mechanics, I would suggest that you not try to meet during the summer. Most people are on and off campus so irregularly during the summer that attendance will be difficult to maintain. You might try to have a social event to keep people in touch, but give your folks a break; it will be good for them.

Small Groups

From time to time, it will be necessary to use small groups to accomplish specific functions of the fellowship. Two generic uses probably cover all the specific instances: task forces to superintend various events and groups set up for training or discipleship purposes.

As we will discuss in the following paragraphs, the fellowship will undertake several activities and events each year to impact the institution. These include such things as bringing in a speaker, hosting a lecture series, placing an advertisement in the student newspaper, and putting on a workshop. In all such instances, a subset of the entire fellowship should be used on an *ad hoc* basis to do the necessary planning and coordinating.

One of the purposes of the fellowship is to help equip members for ministry and for their work within the institution. This purpose can often be accomplished in smaller training or discipleship groups that meet at a separate time from the weekly meeting of the fellowship. For example, a group might be established for a semester to focus on time management principles or to learn how to share the Gospel with students and colleagues. Christian Leadership Ministries is developing a Core Curriculum that addresses the question, "What is a mature Christian professor or staff member?" This document will define the training opportunities that may be undertaken in small groups or in the weekly fellowship.

One final possibility for small groups relates to prayer. In many cases, members will be impressed to pray on a regular basis for campus issues and concerns. It is suggested that a small group be established for this purpose. The prayer group should meet at a time other than the weekly fellowship meeting. Obviously, there shouldn't be **small** groups for prayer, but commitments being what they are, the small group is the way to serve this function. The small group might actually grow into a formal event such as an annual prayer breakfast.

Events

A number of outreach activities have been developed and used by Faculty/Staff Fellowships to impact their institutions. These outreaches are necessary for the vitality of the fellowship. No matter how effective a fellowship is with the weekly meeting, unless the group is reaching out to students and colleagues on a regular basis, it will lose its zest, its reason for being. The outreach activities will be briefly described below with detailed descriptions including how-to instructions later in this section.

Tenure Workshops. Possibly the most effective way we have of reaching out to colleagues involves the Tenure Workshop. The workshop, which is sponsored by the Faculty/Staff Fellowship, presents a detailed and comprehensive strategy for earning tenure. The presentation may be done by a local member of the fellowship or by a speaker from another university. The formal presentation includes a brief challenge to develop in all areas of life (physical, intellectual, social, and spiritual), in addition to the pursuit of tenure objectives. After the formal presentation, professors from the fellowship share insights that relate to individual colleges and departments, as well as to their own tenure experiences. All new faculty are invited to this annual event.

Newspaper Strategies. One of the most effective ways we as faculty and staff have of impacting our campuses for Christ is by identifying ourselves publicly as Christians. One of the most effective ways of accomplishing this is through regular advertising in the student newspaper. These ads are usually half- or full-page ads, strategically placed, that play on a particular theme, e.g., Christmas or Easter; identify the members of the fellowship by academic or staff titles; and indicate availability to counsel interested students and colleagues. Christian Leadership Ministries has engaged an advertising agency to develop attention-getting ads for the ministry, and these are available from ministry headquarters.

Favorite Faculty Events. This outreach event involves students from various Christian organizations who are challenged to invite their favorite professor or staff member to a banquet (breakfast, lunch, or dinner work equally well) honoring "favorite faculty." The invitations given by the students to their invitee clearly indicate that the event has a Christian flavor stating something like, "Campus Crusade for Christ and the Christian Faculty/Staff Fellowship cordially invite you to a breakfast honoring favorite professors. Dr. James Wilson, Professor of Electrical Engineering at the Georgia Institute of Technology, will speak on 'My Search for Significance.'" You might have students introduce their guests, after which Dr. Wilson shares his testimony. Comment cards are used for follow-up.

Lecture(s). Christian Leadership Ministries can suggest a number of academic lecturers available to give evangelistic and apologetic lectures in university settings. These can be effective if planned and advertised well; comment cards are used for follow-up. One particularly effective approach used recently on several campuses is to have a Christian speaker debate an atheist on some topic of general interest, e.g., "Does God Exist?" In some cases, academic departments and campus organizations are beginning to cosponsor these debates and underwriting some or all of the expenses of the debate.

Student Outreaches. A variety of formats are available for enabling the fellowship to reach out evangelistically to various student populations. Outreaches to international student groups using the *JESUS* film in their own language have been used with success, especially when done around a holiday theme such as Christmas or Easter. Several schools are holding an annual orientation for freshmen at which one or more professors share a brief spiritual challenge, Christian student organizations are showcased, and students have an opportunity to interact with Christian professors on an informal basis.

Faculty Forums. Another excellent campus outreach approach is the Faculty Forum, a series of seminars at which members of the fellowship present talks relating the integration of their Christian faith with their academic discipline. The seminars are open to students and faculty. When the speakers are known and respected on the campus and the topics are judiciously chosen, the forum can attract respectable numbers, both Christian and non-Christian.

The Veritas Forum. The Veritas Forum is a takeoff on the Faculty Forum in which nationally known speakers present a series of seminars usually for four or five consecutive evenings. Lunch presentations and afternoon seminars that relate to the general theme of the forum are also held. The level of publicity used for the Veritas Forum generally causes the forum to be the focus of attention on the campus for the week, generating considerable interest and enthusiasm for the various events. The meetings are usually open to the general public, as well as to the campus community.

Worldwide Web Home Pages. A relatively recent innovation for Faculty/Staff Fellowships is the creation of home pages on the Worldwide Web. These sites contain general information about the fellowship and specific information regarding meeting times, places, and program offerings. Additionally, the sites usually have links to the purpose statement and the statement of beliefs of the fellowship. Perhaps the most powerful attribute of these sites is the linkages they afford to individual faculty and staff who are involved in the fellowship; the individual sites provide biographical information on the individual, his or her Christian testimony and position and/or apologetic papers written by the individual. The fellowship home page concept is definitely a high-tech way of reaching colleagues and students with some heavy information.

Fellowship Potlucks. Fellowship Potlucks are a great way of providing fellowship opportunities to professors, staff, spouses, and friends and to expose prospective members to the Faculty/Staff Fellowship in an informal setting. The potlucks are held on either a semester or annual basis, usually at the home of one of the fellowship members. Invitations to such social occasions should either be by telephone or mailed to the homes of members, never passed out in the weekly meeting with the expectation that they will ultimately find their way into the right hands. Arrangements for food and refreshments for these gatherings should be planned by members of the fellowship and spouses or friends. A light program may be offered but is not absolutely necessary.

Having been involved in a fellowship very much like what is described here for many years, I can say that my involvement was the highlight of my career in academia. Sure, it is difficult to involve busy people. Sure, you might catch some grief from the administration, and you might be misunderstood by your colleagues. For sure, you will attempt things that don't work -- sometimes you might even have spectacular failures. But you will also have great successes. You will see students and colleagues come to know the Savior. You will see lives changed in the fellowship and in the institution. You will see your own life changed in the process. The university is one of the hallmarks of Western civilization. Can we abandon it? I think the Christian Faculty/Staff Fellowship is perhaps the only hope for impacting the university for Christ and for good. Surely the university deserves our best efforts. Doesn't the Christian Faculty/Staff Fellowship deserve your commitment?

Now that we have overviewed the concept of the fellowship, including how it functions and what it does, we are ready to describe in detail how to go about organizing some of the outreach events of the fellowship.

8. TENURE WORKSHOPS

One of the principles I have learned in reaching out to colleagues in the university is to minister to them in ways that meet real needs. One of the reasons that "How to Make Better Grades and Have More Fun" talks are such an effective means of reaching students is that nearly all students want to make good grades -- they have a real need. When you think about needs that professors have, two areas immediately come to mind: time management and tenure. Most professors are stressed in the area of time management; this is why outreach strategies using *The Seven Habits of Highly Effective People* and *First Things First* (Stephen R. Covey, A. Roger Merrill, and Rebecca R. Merrill, New York: Simon & Schuster, 1994) are so effective. For most professors in tenure track positions, the tenure process is a formidable prospect. They have a real need for information on how to successfully negotiate the tenure process. And this need represents an opportunity for those who wish to reach their colleagues in the university. Here is how to capitalize on this opportunity.

Every Christian Faculty/Staff Fellowship should be offering a "How to Make Tenure" workshop to all untenured professors on campus on an annual basis. It is usually a simple matter to obtain a list of all new tenure track faculty from the administration. A *personal letter* of invitation should be sent to each new professor well in advance of the actual seminar. Of course, if each new professor could be personally invited by a Christian professor in his or her department or college, this would be even better. The seminar is usually done on a weekday afternoon and requires about two hours. The format for the seminar is flexible but should include a generic presentation on how to make tenure covering such issues as what counts; how to find out what counts; how to allocate time between teaching, research, and service; how to prepare for the reviews; how to develop a good strategy, etc. In my talk, I present a strategy for making tenure that I think is appropriate for any university or college: in the area of service, cheerfully do your share -- *and no more*; in teaching, try to be an excellent teacher; spend all of your remaining time doing research that will lead to refereed publications in the best journals in your field. The seminar could be given by someone with outstanding academic credentials who is brought in from at least 50 miles away (with a briefcase) or by one of the members of the fellowship who has a solid reputation for excellence within the university. My talk is available through the Christian Leadership Ministries Worldwide Web site and may be used as is or modified to suit a particular presenter or campus situation. I would also be happy to assist individuals who wish to develop their own talks.

The seminar can and probably should include comments by senior faculty representing the various colleges on campus to give information that might be specific to individual colleges; e.g., how a concert performance or juried art work might compare with a refereed journal article. It is also quite effective to have younger professors who have recently negotiated the tenure hurdle to share their perspectives: what problems they encountered, what strategies helped them, what they would do differently. If mentoring relationships between established Christian professors and the participants are a possibility, during the seminar is an appropriate time to establish such relationships. Finally, plenty of time should be allowed for Q&A, because there will be many questions. Refreshments might also be served and an informal time for discussion planned. Be sure to have participants provide names and campus addresses for subsequent follow-up.

Follow-up is important and might be accomplished in a variety of ways. At one seminar, the organizer invited interested participants to join a *Seven Habits* discussion group he was starting. All but one of the participants joined the group, and all of them ultimately became involved in the Christian Faculty/Staff Fellowship on that campus. Participants could be followed-up through mentoring relationships that are established as a natural part of the mentoring process. Alternatively, participants might be followed-up by the Christian professor who invited them or by a member of the fellowship who volunteers to do follow-up. And it is, of course, appropriate at the seminar to invite participants to become involved in regular meetings of the fellowship.

I have done several of these workshops in the past several years with uniformly positive results. At the University of Minnesota recently, the organizers were reluctant to try the seminar as a campus outreach strategy, so they decided to have it just for untenured professors involved in the Christian Faculty/Staff Fellowship. The seminar was outstanding in every respect, and the clincher came when a young man who had been denied tenure in an engineering department a year earlier shared why he didn't make tenure. Powerful! One of the senior professors told me after the seminar, "We will be doing this every year at Minnesota, but from now on, we will be inviting *all* untenured professors. At another recent presentation, the Dean of the College of Arts and Sciences attended the seminar and remarked to me before the presentation, "You can't do this. The tenure process is too political, too subjective, too emotional. I just came to see you fall on your face." At the conclusion of the talk, the dean sheepishly commented to me, "I agreed with everything you said! Your recommendations are right on target. Every one of my faculty needs to hear this material!"

The "How to Make Tenure" seminar is one of the most natural and effective ways I know of for reaching out to new professors. Even if someone you invite doesn't come to the seminar for whatever reason, you have created good will because the invitation was extended on behalf of the Christian Faculty/Staff Fellowship. One of the participants at a recent seminar I did wrote on his comment card, "I have been struggling with an out-of-control, unbalanced life for many years and have been thinking about all of this a lot lately. I want to follow most of your suggestions." Meeting real needs. That is what we as Christian professors need to be doing for our colleagues. The tenure seminar does exactly that.

9. NEWSPAPER STRATEGIES

During the years since the beginning of Christian Leadership Ministries, university faculty members and staff who have been involved in the ministry have explored a number of creative ways for using newspapers to communicate an attractive, attention-getting Christian message to students and colleagues alike. The most common approach in this regard is the use of advertisements that play on a particular theme in student newspapers. There are also other, less frequently used, ways of using the printed media to reach out to the university community. Here are a few suggestions that might be helpful.

Newspaper Ads

One of the first ways professors around the country used to reach out to students and colleagues was through advertisements in student newspapers. Walter Bradley and the Faculty Friends group at Texas A&M University deserve credit for coming up with this innovative outreach approach with their first ad which appeared in the A&M newspaper on May 31, 1983, the first day of summer school. The ad had the names of 24 faculty members, and it led with the phrase, "Faculty Friends is a group of faculty who are united by their common experience that Jesus Christ provides intellectually and spiritually satisfying answers to life's most important questions. We wish to make ourselves available to students who might like to discuss such questions with us." I received a copy of the ad in a letter that summer from Mike Duggins, who was our Christian Leadership Ministries staff representative in Texas, and determined to implement a variation of Walter's strategy at my own university. I have in my files the paperwork for our first ad at the University of Alabama. The cover letter is dated Feb. 21, 1984. A copy of our original ad which ran in *The Crimson-White* in the Fall of 1984 is shown in Figure 9-1.

As an aside, when I went to place our first ad in *The Crimson-White*, I recall being pretty nervous knowing the reputation of campus newspapers as fairly liberal. I could imagine all sorts of scenarios, mostly bad, resulting from our desire to purchase ad space for a Christian cause. The young man who helped me place the ad was extremely polite and quite helpful. After I finished giving him the information relating to both the content of the ad and billing, he asked if I could accompany him to the Xerox room to make a copy of the paperwork. As soon as we were out of earshot of his cronies on the newspaper staff, he turned to me and said, "Dr. Mellichamp, you don't know what an encouragement it is to me for you and your colleagues to do this. I am a senior here, and I have pretty much wasted my time at the university drinking and running around. A few weeks ago, I re-committed my life to Jesus, and this is a confirmation to me that I did

THE SOLUTION

The problems we face today both at the societal and individual level are truly awesome. At the national and international level the issues are human rights, nuclear escalation, poverty, and war. At the individual level, people are searching for identity, self worth, acceptance, and love. We believe the solution to all of these problems is Jesus Christ. And we are available to talk to students and colleagues about the Solution

Carrel M. Anderson
Associate Professor of Educational Leadership

Phillip A. Bishop
Assistant Professor of Health, Physical Education, and Recreation

Joann Boshell
Medical Assistant, Russell Student Health Center, GYN

Der-San Chen
Professor of Industrial Engineering

J. Thomas Chesnutt
Associate Professor of Health, Physical Education, and Recreation

Michael H. Finneran
Diving Coach

Charles A. Gibson
Professor of Electrical Engineering

Robert F. Gloor
Associate Professor of Community Medicine

Donna Hawkins
Nurse Practitioner, Russell Student Health Center, OBGYN

Harold R. Henry
Professor of Civil Engineering

T. Allen Henry
Assistant Professor Industrial Engineering

R. Al Leitch
Professor of Accounting

David J. Masoner
Associate Professor of Education

T.H. Mattheiss
Professor of Management Science

Joseph M. Mellichamp
Professor of Management Science

Mark A. Onesi
Assistant Professor of Military Science

John Rasp
Assistant Professor of Statistics

Charles P. Schmidt
Assistant Professor of Management Science

The University of Alabama
Christian Faculty/Staff Fellowship
Dr. Joseph M. Mellichamp
P.O. Box J
University, AL 35486

Robert F. Schuckert
Associate Professor of Human Development and Family Life

Joe F. Smith
Associate Professor of Health, Physical Education, and Recreation

Doru Stefanescu
Professor of Metallurgical Engineering

William H. Stewart
Associate Professor of Political Science

Daniel S. Turner
Associate Professor of Civil Engineering

Nellie C. Vice
Staff Assistant, Civil Engineering

Gary M. White
Assistant Athletic Director

James D. Welker
Professor of Education

Dorian P. Yeager
Associate Professor of Computer Science

Robert T. Anderson
Professor of Education

Figure 9-1. Example of a Student Newspaper Ad.

the right thing. Thanks." Well, so much for bad outcomes. This one encounter was enough to convince me that the newspaper ads are worth whatever effort and cost it takes to do them. And, by the way, one real side benefit of the ads is to encourage Christian students.

The whole idea behind the ad strategy is to have as large a number of Christian professors and staff as possible to endorse Christianity in a public forum on campus. Since most student newspapers are read by many of the students and some of the faculty and staff, this turns out to be a good medium for the endorsement. Ads have been developed for a number of specific occasions and specific issues. For example, groups have done "Welcome Back" ads at the beginning of the fall term to welcome new and returning students to campus after the summer break. Ads that highlight the meaning of Christmas, Valentine's Day, and Easter have been effective, as have ads that come just before exams or Spring Break and which encourage students to think about more than just making it through exams or having a blowout during the break. More recently, we have tried to use ads to address specific issues through a campaign called *Every Student's Choice*, which we will describe later.

Let me describe how you might go about doing this type of outreach on your campus. If you already have a functioning Christian Faculty/Staff Fellowship on campus, the process will be pretty straightforward; if you don't, your first step would be to begin to organize a group along the lines suggested early in this section. As your group (fellowship) begins to come together, you should be able to initiate an ad campaign in the process. If you have a fellowship, the first step in getting started would be to float the idea by the membership and decide whether they would like to engage in this type of activity. Once the decision is made to proceed, you probably should find a member who is willing and available to coordinate the ad strategy for the fellowship on a more or less permanent basis as noted in the "Getting Organized" paragraph of Chapter 7. It will take someone a few hours of work for each ad, so for many fellowships, this has typically been a permanent position. Next, you should determine the level of involvement desired -- most campuses are doing ads on either a semester or an annual basis, although a few are doing several a semester. The ultimate goal, especially of the *Every Student's Choice* campaign, is to do ads more frequently, perhaps even weekly.

Once the level of involvement has been determined, it is appropriate to begin to select the actual ads to be used. Christian Leadership Ministries has numerous examples of effective ads that have been used on other campuses; we also have media experts who are continually developing new ideas. In the past several years, we have provided at least one set of new ads focusing on a particular theme each semester. I suspect the average fellowship has a pretty short planning cycle for ads -- perhaps just the current ad, although it would be desirable from both a budgeting standpoint, as well as for having a comprehensive "marketing strategy" to plan for an entire year. And while we're on the matter of budgeting, you can easily get estimates for the cost of placing the ads from your student newspaper. Rates vary dramatically from school to school, so you need to get a local estimate -- we usually paid about $800 for a half-page ad to run on two consecutive days. While you are checking with the newspaper, also find out what days tend to have the largest readership -- again, this will vary greatly from day to day. For a daily newspaper, Tuesday,

Wednesday, and Thursday are probably best. And finally, try to lock in a good location. Page three or the sports pages worked well for us. It will help in this regard if you know a student who is well-placed on the newspaper staff.

Getting permission of members to put their name and academic or staff title is an absolute must. We recommend using university titles, e.g., Professor of History or Staff Assistant, Student Affairs, rather than departmental affiliations. Also, in order to include only professors and staff who meet some minimum criteria of orthodox Christian beliefs and who have a positive Christian testimony on campus, it is suggested that they sign both a release form and a statement of faith, which can be the statement used by the fellowship (see Exhibit 7-2 for an example). After several years of getting approval for every ad, we decided to go with a permanent form that remains in force until revoked by the individual. This, of course, requires that individuals have some level of confidence in those who are placing the ads or that copy be circulated ahead of time, so that if a member is opposed to a particular ad for whatever reason, he can decline to have his name used. A copy of the release form we used is shown in Exhibit 9-1.

This brings up a point about those who, for whatever reason, might not want to have their name associated with the ad. There are often solid, legitimate reasons why someone might not want to be identified in this way. For example, he might be in a very precarious position from a tenure perspective in a very politically oriented department, in which case it might be appropriate to "lay low" until tenure is assured; at this time, he could become more visible as a Christian. Whatever the reason, there should be no sense of condemnation or criticism from the members of the group who do elect to be identified in the ad. For sure, there will be those who are afraid to come out in such an open way in the university environment. Hopefully, over time they will see that they aren't going to get killed or lose their job and will be encouraged to join the rest of the group.

A few notes on how to maximize the visibility of the ad after it is published. Christian student groups on campus should be notified in advance of publication of the ad, so they can alert their members. Christian students can often use the ads to good advantage in witnessing to their non-Christian friends by turning to the ad in the paper and making a comment along the lines of, "You know, I have suggested to

Exhibit 9-1. Release Forms for Newspaper Ad.

February 21, 1984

Dear Colleague:

Several of us have talked for a number of years about periodically placing an advertisement in *The Crimson-White* identifying ourselves as Christians and indicating a willingness to interact with students and faculty concerning Jesus and Christianity. We are now ready to proceed with this project.

Attached are the following items:

1. Proposed copy for the ad titled "The Solution."

2. The Statement of Faith for the University of Alabama Christian Faculty/Staff Fellowship.

3. A signature sheet indicating agreement with the Statement of Faith and giving approval for using your name with the ad.

If you wish to join us, please sign the approval form and return it to me as soon as possible. Please indicate your exact title as it should appear in the ad.

In Christ,

Rae Mellichamp

Exhibit 9-1. Continued.

Dr. Joseph M. Mellichamp
75 Bidgood

Dear Rae:

I have read the proposed copy for the Christian Faculty/Staff Fellowship ad to be placed in *The Crimson-White*, and I

__ give permission to use my name and title in the ad.

__ would prefer not to be identified with the ad.

_____

Name

_____

Title

If you respond positively, please indicate by your signature, your agreement with the Statement of Faith of the Christian Faculty/Staff Fellowship.

_____

Signature

you that Christianity is intellectually defensible. Here is a list of 40 professors and staff at the university who find Christianity credible." Many of us routinely clip the ads out of the paper, highlight our names with a yellow highlighter, and tape them on our office door or a bulletin board next to our office. Students and colleagues who come to our office will see our name and be impressed to read the ad.

I once had a really funny incident happen as a result of posting the ad on my office door. A colleague of another religious persuasion in my department saw the ad and complained to the department chairman, asking him to make me remove it. The chairman remarked he was sorry that our colleague was offended by the ad, but since my office door was actually part of my office and, thus, my personal property, there really was nothing he could do to make me remove the ad. Our colleague then asked if the same reasoning applied equally to him and his office door -- could he post "stuff" on his door as well. The chairman assured him that as long as he didn't put up anything that was lewd or vulgar, he was perfectly at liberty to post anything he wished on his door. The next morning when we came into the building, this man had posted on his door a list of all the salaries of business school faculty with his low salary highlighted in yellow! People do read ads posted on office doors.

A couple of interesting variations have been used in terms of the individuals whose names are included in the ads. Some schools have included alumni and "friends" of the university, that is, financial supporters who happen to be Christians. Some schools have included the names of trustees or regents who are Christians. I had one professor tell me that he was catching grief from his department chairman, not necessarily from the ads, but just in their relationship in general. He suspected that much of this was a result of his Christian walk in his job situation. Then the Christian Faculty/Staff Fellowship placed an ad in the student newspaper that included the name of a very prominent and very powerful trustee. My friend told me that his chairman's attitude toward him changed dramatically, almost overnight after the ad appeared. Coincidental? I think not.

How are such ads financed? After all, 800 bucks a pop is hardly pocket change. There is a fairly general practice among fellowships that members chip in individually to cover the expenses. Some groups actually assess members $10 or $20 dollars for each ad.

Our practice for many years at Alabama was to simply announce what the ad cost and rely on individuals to contribute as they felt led. One or two people would leave a check for $50 or $100 with our treasurer; several would leave a $20; some would leave a five-dollar bill. Over the years, we underwrote many such activities and events all on the basis of "do what you can," and we always seemed to have enough -- never a surplus, but always enough.

Ads in student newspapers are a wonderful way of working together with our colleagues to present Christianity in attractive ways to the entire university community. If you are not using this approach on your campus, I challenge you to. Years ago, I spoke to a faculty group at a very small college about reaching out jointly as Christians and shared the ad strategy with them. Several months later, I received a copy of the student newspaper from one of the professors; it was hardly more than a mimeographed newsletter. Right in the middle of the front page was a Christian faculty/staff ad listing a dozen or so names of faculty and staff -- in a newsletter! If they can make it work in a mimeographed two-sheet rag, you can do it in your campus daily or whatever you have at your school.

Every Student's Choice

It's pretty amazing how much more effective some of the opposing groups are in getting their message before the university community than Christians. Take a look sometime at the bulletin boards in your building, look at the announcements section of your student newspaper, look at your institution's course offerings (my colleague, Bruce Barrett made me aware of this). Other groups are getting their message across. The Gay, Lesbian, Bisexual Association at Harvard University has placed full-page ads in the Harvard *Crimson* with the statement "Your Gay and Lesbian Friends Welcome You Back to School." The National Gay and Lesbian Task Force has a stated goal to have academic programs on every major U.S. campus by the year 2000. There are currently 500 Women's Studies programs with 30,000 courses in U.S. colleges. Many of these courses are used unabashedly to promote the gay/lesbian lifestyle to college students.

And how are Christians doing at communicating the message of Christianity on the college campus? Not very well. Apart from an isolated ad every semester or so, there is not much being done. In an effort to change this, Christian Leadership Ministries and the Campus Ministry of Campus Crusade for Christ have launched a program called *Every Student's Choice* (*ESC*) by which we hope to change the campus culture by raising the level of awareness of individuals on campus to spiritual issues. To this end, we have engaged media experts who are developing strategies to use the media to get our message before the campus community. A significant thrust of the *ESC* campaign is to use newspaper ads to address relevant campus themes. For example, one series of ads was developed for Valentine's Day that the gays and lesbians have co-opted as National Condom Week. The *ESC* ads contrasted the difference between the casual relationships promoted by the gays and lesbians and the deep, lasting relationships that result from being committed first to the Lord Jesus and then to another person.

The *ESC* ads feature a local telephone number and a Worldwide Web site where the reader can request information relating to the topical focus of the ad. Caller information is relayed to the local campus, so that Christian volunteers can personally provide the requested information and answer any questions that may arise. The *ESC* strategy is not limited exclusively to newspaper ads; it includes posters, take-away materials, and much more. The ultimate aim of the *ESC* strategy is to have a series of issues throughout the academic year for which an attractive Christian position is being presented in the media. In general, the newspaper ads might be placed either with or without faculty/staff names. Thus, for appropriate ads, individual Faculty/Staff Fellowships might be identified in a sponsoring capacity; for other ads, there might be no reference to a fellowship at all. Detailed information on the *ESC* campaign may be obtained from Christian Leadership Ministries headquarters in Dallas.

Letters to the Editor

One effective way of contending in the media is for Christian Faculty/Staff Fellowships to respond to campus concerns through letters to the editor of the local student newspaper. Over the years, we responded many times to a variety of issues including evolution/creation issues, Gay/Lesbian Association funding, homosexual lifestyle issues, and university-sponsored programs. A couple of admonitions are probably in order here. First, there are so many opportunities to respond to different things in the course of a normal year, that it could become a full-time occupation for the entire group. Thus, it is necessary to select one or two issues during the year for which strong Christian positions can be articulated. Second, there is a sense in which these communications tend to turn into long-running debates, and the one who gets in the last word often comes out the winner. Thus, it is important to make the strongest possible case in your response and then to move on to another issue as opposed to continuing to dialog with those who disagree.

The bottom line is that the letters to the editor format is a good forum for speaking out on issues that students and colleagues are asking questions about. Christian thought certainly should be represented in this forum. I have had many professors and staff tell me that they don't read the student newspaper. I believe this is a big mistake. True, much of what one normally finds in the campus rag is trivial and silly. Some of it is pointless. But the campus newspaper does reflect the interests and thinking of the students, and if we are going to contend in the arena of issues, we must know what the issues are. A thoughtful letter to the editor from a few caring professors and staff can have a powerful impact on seeking young minds.

Op-Ed Pieces

For a number of years at Alabama, several members of the Faculty/Staff Fellowship talked about writing a series of articles offering a Christian perspective on a variety of issues for publication in the student newspaper. And for years, that was all there was to it -- talk. Finally, someone, I don't remember who, got tired of the talk and challenged us to "put up or shut up" as the old saying goes. So we asked one of our members, David Sloan, a journalism professor, to lead a three-week (over our lunch meeting) seminar on "How to write for the print media." It is one thing to write an article for a scholarly journal and quite another to write a newspaper article. David did a splendid job, and as a result, several members agreed to spend some time during the summer to write an article. Well, when we came back in the fall, in true professorial fashion, no one had even started his article. But we all felt guilty, and so over the course of the fall semester, seven of us cranked out short essays. Here were our offerings:

- "A Conservative Economist Looks at the 1994 Elections" by Dr. John S. Evans, Professor of Economics
- "Science vs. Faith: An Invented Dilemma?" by Dr. William Keel, Associate Professor of Astronomy
- "Creation: The Biblical Account vs. Science" by Dr. Joseph M. Mellichamp, Professor of Management Science
- "Just Look at Yourself!" by Dr. Phillip A. Bishop, Professor of Human Performance Studies
- "What is? What Should We Do? And Wishful Thinking" by Dr. James P. Cover, Associate Professor of Economics
- "A Short Roadmap to the Human Heart" by Dr. Terry Pickett, Professor of German
- "Evidence for God's Existence is Overwhelming" by Dr. David Sloan, Professor of Journalism

In his seminar, David had encouraged us to think about targeting the articles for the Op-Ed page of newspapers in the region. On March 2, 1995, I sent copies of all seven articles to 28 daily newspapers in Alabama, Georgia, Florida, Tennessee, and Mississippi. This was probably a bad tactical move on my part. We only heard back from one editor that he was publishing one of the articles. Others of the articles might have been published without the editor informing us. I think if we had individually submitted the articles one at a time, we would have had a much higher acceptance rate. Notwithstanding the poor acceptance rate, I still think this is a wonderful idea. Christian professors need to be influencing the culture. Think of what could happen if there was a steady stream of letters from Christian academics appearing in the Op-Ed pages of newspapers around the country.

If you have some good thinkers who like to write in your group, consider improving on this approach.

10. FAVORITE FACULTY EVENTS

An excellent way of communicating the Gospel to colleagues in the university is the "Favorite Faculty Banquet." In this strategy, students from the various Christian student groups on campus -- Campus Crusade for Christ, Navigators, Inter-Varsity, Baptist Student Union, etc. -- are challenged to invite their favorite professors or staff member to a banquet in their honor. The meal may be a breakfast, luncheon, or dinner; all work equally well. The program at the meal includes a time for recognizing and honoring the favorite professors and staff, possibly some light Christian entertainment, and a well-credentialed academic speaker who shares his personal testimony. We have been doing Favorite Faculty banquets in Christian Leadership Ministries circles for at least 15 years with uniformly positive results. I have done a half dozen to a dozen banquets and the comments for all of the affairs I have done have been very positive.

The critical element in doing this type of outreach is the participation of Christian students. If the students get excited about the opportunity and really buy into it, you will have a good turnout; if they don't, you won't. I haven't kept records for the events I have done, but I would venture to guess that the smallest crowd I've seen would be about 50 (20 or so favorite guests and 30 plus students and others involved in hosting the event) and the largest crowd would be well over 100 (with perhaps 50 favorite guests). Even at the low end, I think you would have to agree that this format is an effective way of reaching out to colleagues. As I said, the key is getting students involved. It can be a pretty intimidating thing for a student to (1) invite a professor or staff member to a meal, (2) sit with the guest through a meal and carry on an engaging conversation, and (3) introduce the guest and possibly share why he or she is special. From the professor or staff member's point of view, it is so unusual that a student would show this kind of appreciation, it would be difficult to turn down such an invitation.

If your Faculty/Staff Fellowship decides to do a Favorite Faculty Banquet, the following steps should be addressed when arranging for the event, conducting the event, and doing follow-up after the event.

Arrangements

Well in advance -- possibly several months -- of the anticipated date:

1. Assemble a small group from the Faculty/Staff Fellowship to make arrangements and to oversee follow-up activity.

2. Choose a date and time for the event. Be sure to check the campus calendar to avoid conflicts with another campus happening.

3. Contact the directors of Christian student ministries to enlist involvement of their students. A successful event can be done with involvement of only one of the larger student groups; however, you should try to engage as many of the groups on your campus as possible in the interest of fostering cooperative relations. Remember, this is the key element in the entire endeavor.

4. Line up a speaker for the event, working out details of transportation, honorarium, and local accommodations. Be sure that you get someone with credible academic or professional qualifications and someone who has a reputation as a solid speaker for such occasions. Christian Leadership Ministries has a list of speakers and can help in this task if you need it.

5. Schedule your meeting room, decide on the menu and other physical arrangements.

Some compromise might be necessary to line up the speaker, the meeting room, and the students on the desired date. Once you have completed these steps, you're in business.

A month or so in advance of the event:

1. Have invitations and comment cards printed. These should be attractively done because the invitation will be the visual point of contact between each invitee and the sponsoring groups. Sample invitations and comment cards are shown in Figures 10-1 and 10-2.

> *The students of*
> *Campus Crusade for Christ*
> *and Reformed University Fellowship*
> *and*
> *The University of Florida*
> *Christian Faculty/Staff Fellowship*
> *cordially invite you to their*
>
> ### *Favorite Faculty Breakfast*
>
> *with*
> *Dr. Walter L. Bradley*
> *Professor of Mechanical Engineering*
> *Texas A & M University*
> *Speaking on "True Personal Freedom"*
> *Friday, March 13, 1998*
> *from 7 to 8 a.m.*
> *Ferguson Center Party Room*

Figure 10-1. Favorite Faculty Banquet Invitation.

It is important that the invitation very clearly communicates the Christian nature of the event. This is done by giving the names of the Christian student groups involved, by including the name of the Christian Faculty/Staff Fellowship and possibly the talk title.

2. If desired, arrange financial sponsorship for the banquet. One approach is to let the student pay for his faculty guest and to raise money for scholarships to cover the cost of the student's meal. This enables the student to provide for his guest's meal without making his financial outlay too terribly high.

3. Meet with the Christian student groups to challenge students to bring their favorite professor or staff member to the banquet. If students are concerned about inviting their current professors, have them invite professors from previous semesters. Students who commit to invite a professor should be given an invitation and encouraged to begin praying for the individual they are inviting. Past experience with this format

108

The University of Florida Christian Faculty/Staff Fellowship
Favorite Faculty Breakfast

Please give us your comments on the Banquet and the Program. Thank
you. _____

_____
_____

Would you be interested in talking to Dr. Bradley while he is on campus?
__ Yes __ No

Would you like additional information regarding the University of Florida
Christian Faculty/Staff Fellowship?
__ Yes __ No

Name _____
Address_____ Phone _____

Figure 10-2. Favorite Faculty Comment Card for Follow-up.

suggests that a high percentage of professors who are invited actually
come -- the most frequently cited reason for declining the invitation is a
schedule conflict. Students should be encouraged to actually extend
their invitation about two weeks before the event.

4. Accept reservations from students who have received commitments
from professors or staff members to attend the banquet. Reservations
should be closed a few days before the event, depending on the
requirements of the facility being used. Students should remind their
guests a few days in advance of the event.

5. Carefully monitor activity of students as they are inviting
individuals. If you are going to have a problem at any point, it will be
the students putting off extending invitations and you have a flurry of
activity at the last moment.

6. Enlist participation of as many members of the Christian
Faculty/Staff Fellowship as possible. This will be a faith stretcher for
them as they see colleagues in the university being challenged in an
attractive way to consider the Christian message. It will also be useful
for them to welcome colleagues as they come into the facility and to
help with the follow-up.

The Event

Some pointers for conducting the event are in order.

1. Once the students and their guests have assembled, the Master of Ceremonies (usually one of the leaders in the Christian Faculty/Staff Fellowship) should give a short welcome, especially recognizing faculty and staff guests and complimenting them on being a "favorite" professor or staff member. After the welcome, a blessing should be given by the MC, a student, or a member of the fellowship.

2. When the meal is over or nearly so, the MC should give a general statement of recognition to the favorite faculty and staff guests. One really nice touch that has been done is to have each student introduce his guest and to share why that person is his favorite professor or staff member. This will take a bit of time, but it is worth it. It will be very encouraging for everyone in attendance.

3. The MC should then introduce the speaker, paying particular attention to his academic or professional credentials.

4. The talk should be strongly oriented to academics -- professors and staff -- since they are the honored guests. Moreover, it should include a clear Christian testimony including how one becomes a Christian. At the conclusion of the talk, the speaker should turn the program over to the MC.

5. Follow-up of guests depends critically on how much attention is given to the comment cards. The MC should ask each person to fill out a card, giving his name, address, and campus phone number and comments regarding the meal and program. The comment card may have a place for guests to check if they are interested in meeting with the speaker (if this is possible), if they would like information on the Faculty/Staff Fellowship and/or if they would like to receive Christian material, such as *Mere Christianity* by C.S. Lewis.

6. After the comment cards have been completed, the MC should conclude the banquet.

Follow-up

Follow-up is very important but often neglected. The goal here should be to contact every guest as appropriate to the level of interest indicated on the comment cards. The following steps are recommended:

1. Sort out the student cards and make these available to the leadership of the student groups involved.

2. Sort faculty/staff guest responses into the following categories: Already Christian, Interested, Other.

3. Assign guest cards to fellowship (or program committee) members for appropriate follow-up as follows:

Already Christian. Personally challenge them to become involved with the Christian Faculty/Staff Fellowship.

Interested. Personally meet with each individual for an evangelistic appointment. Delivering written materials mentioned by the MC or the speaker is a good opener. Be sensitive to questions that might have been raised by the speaker.

Other. Send each individual a follow-up letter thanking him for attending and for his support of students. Emphasize the importance of the university as a forum for the exchange of ideas.

A number of years ago, we had Walter and Ann Bradley visit us in Tuscaloosa, Alabama, for a weekend that included a Bama-Texas A&M football game. Our Christian Faculty/Staff Fellowship decided to do a Favorite Faculty Breakfast in conjunction with their visit. We made all the arrangements, reserving a room in the student center for a Saturday breakfast; had invitations and comment cards printed; the whole bit. Then I went and challenged the students, who really got into the spirit of things. I remember imagining how the whole thing would work because it was my first experience with this format. As I speculated about the meeting, I thought about who on campus I would really not want to be invited. Who could be so antagonistic that he might stand up right in the middle of Walter's presentation and create a scene? And I immediately thought of a professor in liberal arts who I thought could present problems, but I thought that the chances of him being invited were so remote that I immediately dismissed the notion. The next day as I was walking into my office, a young woman in my college Sunday School class at church came running up to me shouting, "Dr. Mellichamp, you'll never guess who I invited to the Favorite Faculty Breakfast and who's coming!" In the split second I had to reply, I thought Prof. So-and-So. Then I thought, no way. But, you guessed it. She had invited him, and he was coming.

Well, I spent some anxious moments thinking about all sorts of possibilities, mostly bad. Finally the day arrived. We had a good crowd of about 25 faculty and staff guests and 25 students and four or five representatives from the fellowship. My student was one of the first to arrive with her guest firmly in tow. To my amazement, everything went perfectly. The food was good. The sound system worked. The arrangements were perfect. And Walter did an outstanding job of sharing his testimony with just the right touch of humor in just the right places. The comment cards were completed and collected, and before I knew it, the banquet was over. But not quite. After I declared it officially over, people stayed around and talked and several came up to the front to speak to Walter, including my "friend." He hung around until everyone else had gone and he had a chance at Walter by himself. I eavesdropped to hear what he had to say. I'll never forget it. He said, "You know, Dr. Bradley, you and I have both struggled with some of the same questions. I've come up with a completely different set of answers than you, but I really appreciate you're coming here today and sharing honestly with us. Thanks." So much for my imagined scenario. In fact, the comment cards were all in that same positive light. The students wanted us to do the banquet on an annual basis. The guests were all very favorable in their reactions.

This is such an attractive way of reaching out to colleagues. Every one wins. The students win by doing something special for a professor or staff member who has been special to them. The guests win by being recognized. And the Christian faculty and staff win by having their faith stretched. And the Gospel is shared clearly and attractively. The Favorite Faculty Banquet is easily one of the most effective ways we have of reaching out in the university.

---

11. LECTURES

Another excellent way to reach out to our non-Christian faculty and staff colleagues is through sponsoring a lecture or lectures by outstanding Christian speakers. Experience with this approach has shown there are generally a number of topics that are practically guaranteed to draw a crowd on college and university campuses. And there is a small but growing pool of men and women who are gifted in addressing these topics in public forums. Christian Leadership Ministries maintains a complete list of speakers available for this type of outreach; I will mention a few here:

- "Scientific Evidence for the Existence of God." Dr. Walter L. Bradley, Professor of Mechanical Engineering, Texas A&M University
- "Stephen Hawking, God and the Big Bang." Dr. Fritz Schaefer, Professor of Computational Chemistry, University of Georgia
- "Scientific Evidence for the Existence of God." Dr. Hugh Ross, President, Reasons to Believe
- "Reason in the Balance." Dr. Phillip E. Johnson, Professor of Law, University of California at Berkeley

Of course, there are numerous other speakers and topics that work well for this particular format, these speakers are some of the most popular and effective on the Christian Leadership Ministries circuit. Should you decide to sponsor a lecture or a series of lectures, you would need to make all arrangements by contacting the speaker directly.

When groups of Christian professors and staff do use the lecture or lecture series format approach to reach out to colleagues, follow-up is a key issue and perhaps more time-consuming than all the arrangements that must be done to bring the speaker to campus. Thus, if you should plan to use this approach, it is suggested that you devote careful attention to follow-up activities and have a number of your people trained and ready to carry out this task. You should plan to use comment cards similar to those described in the Favorite Faculty Events chapter and to have the host or Master of Ceremonies ask the audience at the conclusion to fill out the cards giving name, address and comments relating to the talk. Several days after the lecture, you should attempt to personally contact each person who attended. If the lecture attracted a substantial number of students, the local Christian student ministries would probably be happy to follow-up student contacts for you. You should arrange for this possibility in advance of the lecture.

One option with lecture(s) is to have sponsorship by one or more academic departments. We are seeing more and more of this type of arrangement when our lecturers address topics that relate directly to academic disciplines. One thing that academic department sponsorship does for you is to buy credibility. If, for example, you bring in Phillip Johnson to lecture on his book, *Darwin on Trial*, and the biology department co-sponsors the talk, you automatically have bumped the credibility of the lecture to a higher level than if the lecture was sponsored by the Christian Faculty/Staff Fellowship alone. Another really nice thing about doing a lecture jointly with an academic department is that the department will usually pick up some, if not all, of the costs involved with bringing the speaker to campus, including publicity, travel expenses, honorarium, and any facility costs involved. Obviously, we need to become much more intentional in this regard. One wonders how long academic departments will continue to work as allies in our efforts; I suspect that as long as our speakers are lecturing on topics that are in the mainstream of academic pursuits, we will have this opportunity.

One interesting variation on the lecture theme that has proven quite effective on a few campuses is the idea of a debate. The Christian Faculty/Staff Fellowship at the University of Minnesota is now co-sponsoring an annual debate with the atheists and humanists association on the subject "Does God Exist?" In January 1996, I attended the first debate which drew a standing room only crowd of more than 400 in an auditorium designed to seat about 300; probably 200 people were turned away for lack of seats. This year, the event drew 950 people! About 15 percent of those attending requested information about the Christian ministries that sponsored the event. As co-sponsor of the event, the atheist/humanist association underwrote most of the funding for the debate. Now, this is what I call effective. When you can get the opposing forces to underwrite your ministry costs, you are doing something right.

I've always thought it strange that probably the No. 1 way we as Christian professors and staff reach out to colleagues is to invite them to something at church. The last place in the world a non-Christian wants to go is church. Inviting colleagues to a lecture or debate on a topic of general interest to academics is a much more effective way of reaching them for the Savior. There will be plenty of opportunity to get them involved in church after they meet Jesus.

12. FACULTY/VERITAS FORUMS

A variation of the lecture approach to outreach that is unique enough to warrant separate treatment is the lecture forum. Two different formats have been used on many campuses with good results in terms of raising the general level of awareness of spiritual issues on campus and generating contacts from faculty and staff. These formats are the Faculty Forum and the Veritas Forum.

The Faculty Forum

The Faculty Forum is basically a series of lectures sponsored by the Christian Faculty/Staff group; each lecture is given by a Christian professor or staff member who usually is a member of the fellowship. The lectures typically have a common theme, but they reflect the various academic disciplines or research interests of the individual presenters. For example, several years ago, the Christian faculty and staff at the University of Wisconsin launched a series called "I Dissent." The individual talks and presenters were:

- "You Can't be Both a Christian and a Humanist: I Dissent." Professor Mary Lou Daniel, Spanish and Portuguese
- "The Judeo-Christian Ethic is at the Center of Our Ecological Crisis: I Dissent." Professor Calvin DeWitt, Institute for Environmental Sciences

- "To a Scientist, God is an Unnecessary Hypothesis: I Dissent."
  Professor Wayne Becker, Botany
- "Pie in the Sky and Free Enterprise on Earth: I Dissent." Professor
  J. David Richardson, Economics
- "To Err is Human, to Forgive is not My Thing: I Dissent." Professor
  Robert D. Enright, Psychology
- "The Solution to AIDS is Safe Sex and More Research: I Dissent."
  Professor Archie A. MacKinney, Medicine

     The lectures are usually scheduled weekly at the same time and location and are open to everyone in the university community. This format has been followed on different campuses including Texas A&M, where the idea actually originated, and the University of Illinois. The faculty and staff at the University of North Texas recently held a series titled "The Last Lecture Series: What Some of Your Favorite Professors Would Say if Given One Last Opportunity." One of the talks in this series was "Thou Shalt not Bear False Witness Against the Religion of Thy Neighbor." You can see that part of the success of this format is in the use of catchy titles for the talks.

     Another interesting variation of the Forum Format was initiated by a dormitory Resident Adviser at Purdue University. This young woman put together a panel of professors to discuss issues of interest to students as part of the dormitory's enrichment series. She made sure that the Christian faculty was well-represented on the panel. The program allows each panel member to make individual remarks to the issue being discussed, and then has the panel field questions from the audience. The program has been done for a couple of years: it works well and draws a large crowd of students. Since Resident Advisers in many university settings are required to have a certain number of enrichment programs each year for residents, and residents are encouraged to attend the programs, this is a good venue for getting Christian ideas in the marketplace. This is the kind of creative approach that Christian professors and staff need to be taking on their campuses. We can learn from our students -- my hat is off to the R.A. who initiated this approach!

     As is the case with single lecture outreaches, follow-up is also a key for Faculty Forums. The basic follow-up strategy outlined for

Favorite Faculty Events is applicable here with minor modifications because of the recurring nature of the talks.

The Veritas Forum

The Veritas Forum, which originally began at Harvard University, is similar to the Faculty Forum with some important differences. Veritas is a Latin word meaning Truth. The concept behind the Veritas Forum is to focus attention of the university community on issues that relate to truth. The Veritas Forum accomplishes this with a week-long series of seminars given by some of the most outstanding scholars in the country. The forum is heavily advertised in student and local newspapers and other media, including banners in prominent campus locations and hundreds of posters before and during the actual week of meetings. Each week night, Monday through Thursday, there is a plenary talk presented by one of the featured speakers. These sessions are open to the campus community and to the general public. In past Veritas Forums, these have averaged nearly 1,000 people per session. There is usually a luncheon of some sort each weekday that will include a talk for more general campus audiences by one of the featured speakers, as well as afternoon seminars that tend to be a bit more oriented to a particular discipline or interest area within the campus community. For example, most forums have had one luncheon directed toward international students and faculty. Often the afternoon sessions are hosted by a particular department in the institution.

Here is the schedule of evening talks for the Veritas Forum held at Ohio State University in the fall of 1994. The overall theme of the talks was "Truth on Trial."

- "Darwin on Trial: Can You Trust the Argument for Evolution?" Professor Phillip Johnson, Professor of Law, University of California at Berkeley
- "The Bible on Trial: Can You Trust What it Says About Jesus?" Professor Edwin Yamauchi, Professor of History, Miami University
- "Faith on Trial: OSU Christian Faculty Speak Out." A panel of Ohio State University Professors

- "Freud on Trial: Can You Trust Your Thoughts About God?" Professor Paul Vitz, Professor of Psychology, New York University
- "Relativism on Trial: Can You Trust Your Philosophy about Life?" Professor Peter Kreeft, Professor of Philosophy, Boston College

To date, Christian Leadership Ministries has been involved in almost two dozen of these forums. Several campuses have done more than one forum. I was privileged to be an afternoon seminar speaker at the University of Florida's first Veritas Forum in 1996. I remember walking around campus seeing Veritas Forum banners and posters plastered all over the place. There were ads and editorials in the student newspaper. It was as though the entire attention of the campus was focused on the events of the forum. I realize that my impressions were biased by my involvement, but going beyond my bias, there was an incredible amount of media directing attention to the forum events. There was an air of excitement I have seldom experienced in the large auditorium that was the venue for the evening talks. Every night for four nights, there were large crowds for the talks -- many students, but also many adults as well, either university faculty and staff or people from the Gainesville community. The question-and-answer times for the evening talks were interesting and reflected that many of those in the audience were seeking answers to life's difficult questions. Many apparently had rejected religious solutions and were looking for something more.

Obviously, such an undertaking requires much in the way of manpower and financial resources. The more successful Veritas Forums have had the involvement of many Christian student organizations and many local churches, with all groups contributing both manpower and finances. If you decide to take on a Veritas Forum, you should contact Christian Leadership Ministries for detailed information on how to organize and plan for the event. There is also a charitable organization that will underwrite some of the costs involved with getting speakers -- honoraria and travel expenses.

13. SPEAKERS BUREAU

In our Christian Faculty/Staff Fellowship meetings at the University of Alabama, we would frequently come up with ideas that would enable us to impact the university for Christ -- this should not be surprising; this is precisely the purpose of the fellowship. In fact, we usually had more ideas floating around than we had manpower to execute. One idea kept resurfacing every year or so until about its fifth appearance, Bob Brooks got tired of hearing us talk about it and decided to take it on himself. The idea was a Christian speakers bureau. We felt like many of the Christian campus organizations and local churches could possibly use Christian professors and staff in speaking situations from time to time, but most of them probably didn't have access to information about which faculty and staff were available for speaking engagements and the topics which could be addressed. So we decided to put together a list of our members who could speak, along with some biographical information and a list of topics, and to periodically circulate this list to the organizations we thought might benefit from it.

Bob published our first listing in March 1994 and sent copies to about a dozen campus organizations and churches. Here are a couple of entries from that list:

Dr. A. Eugene Carden, Ph.D., P.E.
Professor of Engineering Science and Mechanics
219 Hardaway Hall
Tuscaloosa, AL 35487-0278
(205) 348-xxxx
Biographical Sketch:
Engineering professor specializing in materials, mechanics, design and failure analysis.
Topics:
Creation/Evolution
Old Testament Survey
Metallurgy and the Bible

Dr. William C. Keel, Ph.D.
Associate Professor of Astronomy

206 Galilee Hall
Tuscaloosa, AL 35487
(205) 348-xxxx
Biographical Sketch:
Astronomer and astrophysicist. Has worked with many of the world's most powerful optical and radio telescopes and satellite observatories, such as the Hubble Space Telescope. Specializes in galaxies and their interactions.
Topics:
An Astronomer Looks at Genesis

If your group decides to publish something like this as a service to Christian campus organizations and churches, you should be willing to make a long-term commitment. The list should be updated annually as university people come and go, thus, the people and topics will change from year to year. A one-shot publication is probably not going to generate a lot of speaking engagements for your members, but as leaders of campus organizations and churches get an updated list every year, they will begin to use it in planning their organizational calendars. So you are looking at a two- to three-hour project every year for which someone in your group would assume responsibility.

The flip side of this is that some of us were concerned if we did such a listing, we would be deluged with requests to speak, something that you don't relish if you are already busier than you want to be. We prepared for this eventuality by informing members who were listed that they would be responsible for deciding how much speaking they could do and for making the arrangements for their talks with the requesting organizations. This concern did not materialize, although some of our members did get requests as a result of the list being published.

So, there you have it. A nice, neat byproduct of Christian professors and staff meeting together on a regular basis to address the issue of how they can have an impact for Christ in their university situation. This idea was entirely the result of the creative research and development effort of our Christian Faculty/Staff Fellowship.

14. STUDENT OUTREACHES

Over the years, we have seen Christian faculty and staff groups come up with some wonderful ways of reaching out to students on campus. Here are two of the most frequently mentioned approaches. The first is an orientation for incoming students and the second is related to international students.

Freshmen Orientation

Several years ago in our fellowship, James Cover, a professor in the Economics Department who did his doctoral study at the University of Virginia, mentioned that there was a Christian professor at Virginia who held an orientation for all new students at the university each year. Apparently, this professor was highly respected on campus and had a track record for dispensing valuable information, including a word of Christian testimony, so he was able to attract a large crowd every year. James was so impressed with comments he heard about this professor at Virginia that he prevailed on our group to consider trying an orientation for freshmen.

As we kicked this idea around, we decided it would be good to have as many members from our fellowship attend as possible. We would promote the program as a time when students could meet some of their professors "up close and personal." (You might recall that this was the sound bite the TV network used covering the 1992 Winter Olympics whenever they would feature an Olympic athlete.) In the program, we would have a few professors from our group briefly share on some appropriate theme: encouragement to do well in studies, how important the spiritual dimension is during the college experience, whatever. Then we would have each of the Christian student ministry directors introduce his ministry and explain how the students could get involved. After that, we would all mingle with the students and have an informal time of conversation and refreshments. Figure 14-1 is a copy of the flier we printed up to advertise the event.

As I imagined the meeting unfolding, I could see 200 or so freshmen milling around in the Capstone Dining Room of our student center. If we mobilized every member on our list, there would only be

```
┌─────────────────────────────────────────┐
│                                         │
│          STUDENT                        │
│                                         │
│       ORIENTATION                       │
│                                         │
│                                         │
│  WHO:     ALL UA STUDENTS               │
│  WHAT:    MEET SOME OF YOUR PROFESSORS  │
│           UP CLOSE AND PERSONAL. FIND OUT│
│           HOW TO MAKE YOUR COLLEGE YEARS│
│           COUNT. DRINK COKES AND EAT OREOS.│
│  WHEN:    WEDNESDAY, SEPTEMBER 15, 1993.│
│           8:00 - 9:00 P.M.              │
│  WHERE:   FERGUSON STUDENT CENTER,      │
│           CAPSTONE DINING ROOM (1ST FLOOR).│
│                                         │
│                                         │
│             SPONSORED BY:               │
│    THE UNIVERSITY OF ALABAMA CHRISTIAN  │
│        FACULTY/STAFF FELLOWSHIP         │
│                                         │
└─────────────────────────────────────────┘
```

Figure 14-1. Freshmen Orientation Flier.

35 Christian professors and staff members. I thought the students might have a difficult time finding the professors and staff to meet them up close and personal. So I thought it would be a great idea to have a bunch of white baseball caps with "UA Christian Faculty/Staff Fellowship" embroidered in crimson on the front and have each member of our group to wear one of the hats. When I shared this idea with the group, they all thought it was about the stupidest thing they had ever heard. Unfortunately (or fortunately), I had already ordered 25 hats -- we were on a pretty tight schedule, and I had to order first and get permission later. Well, they vowed they weren't going to wear the hats, PERIOD.

Our plan for promoting the event was simple. We would put a small ad in the student newspaper, but we would do the bulk of our promotion by passing out fliers the afternoon of the meeting at a function the university has every fall where incoming students come to the University Quad to find out about and sign up for student organizations. Bad mistake! The day of the orientation, it started raining in the early morning and rained all day -- I'm talking typhoon rain, not just the light stuff. The university function was canceled until a later date, and with it, our opportunity to pass out our fliers. But we had already reserved the room, along with 250 Cokes and about 40 dozen Oreo cookies.

Earlier in the week, I had sent out an intracampus mail memo telling our members that we were all out on a limb and that if we didn't have a big showing of professors and staff, we would all be embarrassed. Wow! Did the memo ever work. We had 30 of our people show up 30 minutes before the orientation to be briefed -- we had never had that many people show for any event. And I had the 25 baseball caps. I've never seen anything like it before or since. They fought like animals over the hats! Those who were successful in getting one said later that the hats were definitely one of my best ideas of all time. In fact, they thought that we should get embroidered golf shirts and windbreakers -- what a simple way to communicate to others that you are a Christian.

We spent $400 for white baseball caps, Cokes, and Oreo cookies. And we had **four** students show up for the orientation! Here is a good question for you. Is a college freshman worth a hundred bucks? Of course! What did we do? We went ahead with the program just as if there had been 200 students there. And we had a great time. Joe Smith, a professor in the College of Education, was the first to share and he made a comment about how his father had raised him better than to wear a hat indoors and he was only doing it because I said he had to. The faculty and staff testimonies were all right on target. The student ministry directors gave their pitch. And then we hit the Cokes and Oreo cookies. The four students had a great time! They didn't have any trouble finding the professors and staff. Each of the students had a little crowd of folks in white baseball caps standing around listening to him. One of the students was a French major and she got to meet Michael Picone, a professor in the French Department, who is a Christian. One student wanted to go for a Ph.D. in mathematics and become a Christian math professor, and he got to meet one of our members who was a professor in the Math Department, as well as a Christian. As we left after everyone had run out of gas, we each had a couple of six-packs of Cokes under our arms and a couple of dozen Oreos in a sack. The following week at our regular meeting, we all agreed the orientation had been one of the best things we had ever done. My colleagues loved the hats -- some of us still wear them. They loved the format. Everything was perfect except for one large detail: we blew it in our promotion! But everyone wanted to do it again the following year, including the four students and all of the student ministry directors. Unfortunately, some of the folks in our group who organized the event were not able to pick it up again the following year and it didn't happen. Members of our fellowship still refer to it as "Mellichamp's deal with the baseball caps," but they always smile when they say it.

This is a winner. Several schools have contacted me since then and were interested in doing something similar. I'd like to know if anyone has pulled it off. It took a lot of planning to do the first time; I think if done on an annual basis, it would be a piece of cake.

International Students

Another natural student outreach option for the Christian Faculty/Staff Fellowship focuses on international students. Several variations on this theme have been tried with good results. The most common format involves showing the *JESUS* film to a target group of international students, usually in conjunction with an American holiday. The *JESUS* film is a full-length motion picture of the life of Christ based on the Gospel of Luke produced by Warner Brothers. The film is available from Campus Crusade for Christ in more than 200 languages in either 16 mm or video format. Most versions have an invitation for the viewer to pray to accept Christ at the conclusion of the film, although the film could be stopped before showing this section. The film can be shown in conjunction with a traditional holiday meal or a reception. When a meal is done, it is usually served first, followed by the film screening; when a reception is done, it can be done either before or after the film.

Since most major universities and colleges have a sizable international student population and many professors have contact with international students either as graduate students or in classroom situations, this outreach format is a good one. Many international students are curious to learn about the American culture and traditions, but many of them don't have much opportunity to do so. This approach affords them an opportunity to interact with Americans and to learn about Christianity in a non-threatening atmosphere. The ideal approach to doing this type of outreach is to have involvement of many Christians who personally invite internationals and either meet them at the location or arrange to pick them up and attend the event with them.

This type of activity is fairly easy to do, and requires very little in terms of organizational effort. If your group decides to try this, you will need to arrange for a suitable location, a copy of the film and associated projection equipment, the meal or refreshments (if desired), and work out some scheme for inviting students -- printed invitations, letters, etc. That's about it. Of course, the critical event, as is true for most of our evangelistic efforts, is in the inviting. If you do a good job of involving members of the fellowship and they do a good job of inviting students, you will have a good turnout. If not, you may be eating a lot of turkey!

One of the most ambitious implementations of this strategy, was sponsored by the Faculty Christian Fellowship and other Christian organizations at the Ohio State University a year or so ago. Following is a copy of the announcement which was sent to faculty and staff.

"Would you please share this information with your groups and faculty members? Please use this as an opportunity for you to reach out to international students."

"There will be a special showing of the *JESUS* film in different languages including Chinese, Japanese, Hindi, Thai, Spanish, Russian, Indonesian, Korean, and English on Saturday, March 30th, at 7 p.m. This is shown in connection with the Easter holiday which takes place one week later. Locations are as follows:

Chinese	Royers Activity Center Multipurpose Room
English	Royers Activity Center North Room
Japanese	Ohio Union Buckeye A (3rd Floor)
Spanish	Ohio Union Buckeye C (3rd Floor)

Russian	Ohio Union Buckeye E (3rd Floor)
Indonesian	Ohio Union Buckeye G (3rd Floor)
Thai	Ohio Union State Room (3rd Floor)
Korean	Ohio Union Board Room (3rd Floor)
Hindi	Ohio Union Gray Suite E (Basement)

The film will be shown at the same time at all locations. Some of the showings will be on video monitors."

"This film is the most popular movie ever made. It has been seen by more than 500 million people. It has been translated into more than 200 languages. It is a full-length feature film that is 120 minutes long."

"There will be a reception following the films to enjoy meeting others who attend. There is NO COST for the film or the reception."

"This special film festival is being sponsored by International Friendships and Bridges International, groups seeking to promote friendship and hospitality for international students and scholars. We work closely with volunteers from local churches. Our activities are open to students from all cultures and religious backgrounds."

Approximately 300 international students attended the event at Ohio State with 15 indicating they made a commitment to Christ at the conclusion of the screening. Of course, the participating organizations benefited from having contact with the international students who came to the event.

This is such an attractive way to reach out to a special group of students, and it is so simple to organize, it should be a regular part of your Faculty/Staff Fellowship's outreach activities. If you have never considered doing a showing of the *JESUS* film for international students, you should.

15. WORLDWIDE WEB HOME PAGE

One of the fun things about Christian Leadership Ministries is to see what happens when an idea catches on. This is what happened when the student newspaper ads first started. Within a year of the first appearance at Texas A&M University, ads were cropping up in student newspapers all over the country. This is what happened with the Tenure workshop idea. And this is what is happening with Worldwide Web home pages. We don't know exactly where and when the first Christian Faculty/Staff Fellowship home page came on-line -- we think it was the University of California at Santa Barbara in the spring of 1996, but Indiana State University and Penn State University have also laid claim to being first. Whoever thought of it, it is a great idea, and it doesn't matter who gets the credit as long as the Lord gets the glory. If you have a Christian Faculty/Staff Fellowship, you need to have a home page.

Simply stated, a home page is a location for general information about a Christian Faculty/Staff Fellowship and specific information relating to activities and members of the fellowship. Let me describe the home page for UCSB and you'll get the idea. The title is FACULTY/STAFF CHRISTIAN FORUM followed by the phrase "Let There Be Light." Below this is a fragment of Michelangelo's painting from the Sistine Chapel -- this is a really nice touch of class that grabs one's interest. The remainder of the first page is a table of contents that presents the user with the following options:

Info Q&A. This section contains basic Christian apologetic information presented in a question-and-answer format.

Recommended Reading. Current books of interest to Christian academics are highlighted.

Bible Study. An investigative Bible study answering the question "Who is Jesus?" is included.

Faculty & Staff at UCSB. A brief history of the Faculty/Staff Christian Forum at UCSB is given here and the current membership as shown on the most recent newspaper ad.

Info Calendar. This section contains the calendar for the current quarter including meeting topics, speakers and locations, as well as meeting times.

News. Included here is information relating to events and conferences that might be of interest to Christian academics.

Library. The library section contains references to various articles of interest to users under several categories including: economics, education, history, mathematics, and philosophy.

Related Web Sites. This section gives addresses of other Web sites including Christian Leadership's Leader U, Campus Crusade for Christ's site, and sites for several Christian ministries at UCSB.

The UCSB site was made possible by Christian Leadership's *1996 Erick Nilson* grant to Professor Jeffrey B. Russell and is a fine example of excellence in presenting Christianity to the academic community, which we should be striving for in our outreach efforts. Spend some time and browse through this home page. I suspect that many students and faculty colleagues at UCSB and at other places have stumbled onto this location and come away with a very different impression of Christianity. If your fellowship doesn't already have a home page on the Web, don't waste another moment. Identify a person in your group with good computer skills, tell him to check out the UCSB site and some of the other examples of fellowship Web sites (which can accessed from the Christian Leadership Ministries Website -- http://www.leaderu.com), and see what happens.

---

16. FELLOWSHIP POTLUCKS

One of the two major purposes of the Christian Faculty/Staff Fellowship as stated earlier is to minister to the faculty and staff who constitute its membership by promoting relationships between and among them. And one of the best ways of fostering relationships between and among members is to periodically plan social gatherings for them. Probably the most appropriate type of social activity is one that is familiar to most professors and staff: the potluck dinner. At the University of Alabama, we tried to have an annual gathering, either around Christmas or at the end of the academic year at the home of one of the members. Speaking from experience, it is usually much better to let the women members of the fellowship and the wives of male members plan and deliver on this option. I think once or twice, some of the men in our group tried to pull this off with near disastrous results. On one particular occasion, my wife, Peggy, Bob Brooks, and I were the only guests to show up, and I'm not really sure that our hostess learned of the event too much in advance of our arrival at the door. After that, we let the real pros take over and had some really great times together.

The usual way of coordinating these events is to let the hostess provide the meat dish (which may be purchased by the fellowship) and perhaps the drinks and let the others bring dishes after consultation with the hostess as to what dishes will work together. I'm sure that it is not quite as easy as this, but this is my simplistic understanding of how it all comes together.

In addition to the meal, it is appropriate to have a speaker, if one is available. Peggy and I have spoken on the topic "Ministering Together as a Couple" at potluck dinners for fellowships. Some light entertainment is also in order followed by a time for conversational prayer directed to campus concerns. One thing we did at several potlucks that was fun and helped us get to know one another was to have each couple share how they met and give a brief history of their life together. Phil Bishop always had some outlandish story about how he met Brenda that thoroughly embarrassed Brenda who is a real sweetheart and had the rest of us rolling on the floor. Of course, none of his stories contained even a grain of truth; he made them up simply for the shock effect and to break the ice, and did they ever do that. Another thing you might do is have each person share just a bit of his personal testimony; this should be done advisedly as there might be non-Christian guests or some of the regulars might not feel comfortable with this type of sharing. Just exercise some sensitivity if you do this; it can be very encouraging to see how uniquely God has worked in the lives of your associates.

Joe and Jane Mulvihill, our Christian Leadership Ministries colleagues at the University of Minnesota, have done a wonderful job of using the potluck to foster relationships in their fellowship. They have a potluck every quarter during the school year. They usually have some fun entertainment -- the time we were there, they had one of the faculty wives who does a clown act perform, and she was quite good. They usually have a speaker. On at least two different occasions, they have had the event at the home of the university president (two different individuals) and have had the president address the group on a topic pertaining to the role of Christians in the university. The potlucks at Minnesota are well-attended because the members are forming close bonds within the group, and they enjoy one another's company; the two dinners at the president's home were booked. This hasn't happened by accident. It happened because Joe and Jane made it a priority and built this event into the fellowship's quarterly schedule.

The fellowship potluck is a great way to build relationships in your group. It is also a good way to introduce potential members to the group in a non-threatening, fun way. If your group is not currently functioning in this way or if you are not doing it in a consistent way, I would encourage you to find someone in the group who enjoys this type of activity and make him or her the Czar or Czarina of potlucks. Just be sure to send all invitations to the home address rather than the office. If you break this simple rule, you may be in for a rude awakening!

There are many different ways of ministering together with Christian faculty and staff colleagues on the university campus. Of course, the first step in this type of ministry is to organize a Christian Faculty/Staff Fellowship. True, you can do some of the ministry activities we have covered in this section without having a weekly fellowship. I know of several campuses that do newspaper ads and bring in outside speakers and even Veritas Forums without a weekly fellowship. But, let's face it, the folks involved at this level are basically carrying out events that someone else is proposing to them. There is no real movement in the sense of individuals who have a commitment to seeing the institution changed and to seeing colleagues and students come to Christ. There is no opportunity to address campus concerns as they arise and to formulate and implement strategies to address some of the issues. I think of our group at the University of Alabama, and we truly functioned in the think tank mode. The fellowship concept and form was hammered out by our group. The idea of the tenure workshop came from our group. So did the idea for the speakers bureau, the freshmen orientation, and the Op-Ed newspaper strategy. We stumbled a bit; we fell flat on our face at times. But we had a movement of folks who wanted to have an impact for the Savior.

Possibly the best illustration I know of this occurred a year ago, well after we had left Tuscaloosa and moved to Atlanta. In January 1996, officials at the University of Alabama announced that the National Gay and Lesbian Association was holding its annual conference at the university -- in violation of state laws. The state of Alabama has laws that prohibit organizations that advocate breaking state laws from using state facilities. Alabama has laws against sodomy. But the contracts were signed, and the rooms reserved; when the announcement was made, the arrangements were a done deal. When the Christian Faculty/Staff Fellowship heard the news, they started discussing what might be an appropriate response from the group. And here is what they decided.

The Christian Faculty/Staff Fellowship set up a hospitality suite for conference delegates at which they served soft drinks and cookies. They also had a prayer room during the sessions so that Christians from the community could come and pray for the delegates. Imagine having the following announcement in each of the conference sessions: "There is a hospitality suite in Room 201 sponsored by the University of Alabama Christian Faculty/Staff Fellowship." Members of the Tuscaloosa community found out what the fellowship was planning and offered to be involved in the prayer effort and to help with the expenses of providing refreshments. At the conclusion of the conference, the conference chairwoman told Phil Bishop, who is the leader of the fellowship at Bama, "I'm going to have to rethink my position on Christians, because this just doesn't fit the mold!" What an attractive way to contend for the faith on the university campus! This is what can happen when there is a mobilized group of Christian faculty and staff seeking to have an impact for Christ in the institution.

So your first priority is the weekly fellowship. Once you get that going smoothly, you can begin to reach out in some of the ways outlined in this section. And when you really start functioning in the think tank, research and development mode you can begin to develop strategies specifically for your unique campus situation. Then you will begin to impact the institution for Christ; you will start to see colleagues and students influenced for the Savior. We will have to publish a second edition of this manual including the ideas you and your associates have implemented.

PART THREE:

MINISTERING NATIONALLY AND INTERNATIONALLY

We had a dean once at Alabama whose hobby was collecting sayings. He had been doing this for a long time and he had a saying for almost every occasion. One of his favorites was a Bible verse that he used to justify travel budgets for his faculty and, of course, it became near and dear to our hearts because we were the beneficiaries of the funds he raised by quoting it. He never gave the complete citation (I think deans can get away with this), but did say it was from the book of Daniel. I looked it up with help from my concordance because he had taken some executive liberty in his paraphrase of it. "They traveled to and fro across the land, and knowledge increased." Daniel 12:4 While Dean Mitchell was referring to scholars traveling to academic conferences, I think the inference can be applied to academic people in general. We do travel a lot. And as a consequence, those of us who are Christians often have opportunities beyond our own universities.

I mentioned earlier the impact on my view of my career Acts 1:8b has had, "And you shall be My witnesses both in Jerusalem; and in all Judea and Samaria, and even to the remotest part of the Earth." When I first started thinking about using my influence as a Christian professor, I was pretty well focused on the University of Alabama -- my Jerusalem. But as I tried to be faithful in reaching out in my university, God opened up opportunities for me to have an influence for Him in an ever-expanding circle. And I have traveled to represent Him on many occasions, literally "in the remotest parts of the Earth." I just returned from meetings in Western Europe where the international leadership of Campus Crusade for Christ discussed how we could establish a ministry presence on every major university campus in the world! That is pretty much a world vision.

I think the principle applies in general: as we are faithful in our Jerusalem, the Lord expands our borders and sends us farther and farther from there as His representatives. I think the principle is especially true for those of us in academe. In this section, I want to outline a number of ministry opportunities you have as you begin to look beyond the borders of your own university or college campus.

17. CHRISTIAN LEADERSHIP MINISTRIES INVOLVEMENT

I don't know about you, but for me, one of the most difficult aspects of being a Christian in the secular university has always been to keep my focus, to maintain a clear vision of what I believe God has called me to be and do. There is so much pressure from the job: pressure to be a good classroom teacher, pressure to conduct cutting-edge research and to publish, pressure to be involved in service activities. Add to that the demands of family life and church activity and possibly some involvement in the community, and it is enough to swamp the most well-organized and disciplined individual. And if that were not enough, there aren't often too many people around you in the university who have a similar sense of calling, who are seeking to have an impact for Christ on the campus. Most of your colleagues are probably very intent on their careers. Many of them are not believers and most who are believers have never seriously considered Christ's command to be His witness in the university. Given this environment, maintaining a sense of perspective and a clear vision is difficult. As the faculty ministry of Campus Crusade for Christ, Christian Leadership Ministries can help you in a couple of important ways in this regard.

Christian Leadership Ministries Conferences

This is why I am such a fan of the various conferences that Christian Leadership Ministries sponsors both regionally and nationally. I mentioned earlier how Walter and Ann Bradley and Peggy and I met together every summer for several years at Campus Crusade for Christ's summer staff training conference in Fort Collins, Colorado. Since about 1982, Christian Leadership Ministries has hosted the National Faculty Leadership Conference -- a week-long training time for Christian professors and academic staff -- every other year in conjunction with Campus Crusade for Christ's staff training. These times have been for me like a routine battery charge. We have often driven or flown into

Colorado much like a battered dog with his tail between his legs -- worn out from the pressure of the job and tired from the challenge of trying to live Christianly in the secular university. How those conferences have restored my vision and revitalized my enthusiasm for what the Lord has charged me to accomplish and to be for Him! Just being with other academics who have the same calling and who are facing the same challenges; hearing the inspirational speakers and uplifting music; and stepping away from the job for a few days to assess and re-evaluate things and to re-focus my direction has been the difference between persevering and falling by the wayside. By the end of the week, I am ready and raring to get back on campus, armed with new ideas and refreshed in my spirit -- with all the energy and enthusiasm of a young puppy.

I'm not surprised that many of my colleagues in academia burn out after a few years in action. The daily grind will do that to you. If you are a Christian professor or staff member, you need to take advantage of the regional and national conferences we host through Christian Leadership Ministries. Carve out the time; set aside the funds. Take your spouse; take your children. Some of the happiest times we had as a family when our children were growing up were summers with Campus Crusade for Christ. We still talk about the time we drove to Cuernavaca, Mexico, for summer training. What an experience! In fact, my daughter, Jennifer, called Peggy just a week or so ago and told her that she has recently been reflecting about how rich her life has been and of the wonderful memories she has of traveling around with us (mostly on Christian Leadership Ministries/Campus Crusade for Christ related trips). If you have not been participating in these regional and national vision and training opportunities, you are really missing out; come join us. I'll be there!

Faculty Affiliates

Like the U.S. Marines, Christian Leadership is looking for a few good men and women. We will never have enough full time staff to get the job done. There are more than 3,000 colleges and universities in the U.S. and the leadership of Campus Crusade for Christ has targeted 2,000 major universities internationally. There needs to be a Christian faculty/staff effort on every one of these campuses. Guess how many staff we currently have in Christian Leadership Ministries? Would you believe 100? A hundred staff to reach 3,000 campuses here and 2,000 abroad! No way! It isn't going to happen. Unless we find men and women who will join us and take responsibility for their own part of the harvest field -- for their own university or college campus. We literally need to see hundreds of men and women who will step out and say, "I will be the point man or woman on my campus. I will trust God to raise up a faculty/staff ministry here. I'm your man. I'm your woman. I don't know exactly what will emerge or how it will happen, but I will assume responsibility to be the catalyst to see God do it."

We are challenging men and women with this mindset to become Christian Leadership Ministries Faculty Affiliates. And I don't know of a better way to maintain perspective and to keep a clear vision before you than to join Christian Leadership Ministries as a Faculty Affiliate. As an Affiliate, we in Christian Leadership Ministries will come alongside you and help you to "see your campus through God's eyes" -- to envision how the Lord might use you and your colleagues to have an impact for Him there. We will provide you with the training and the resources necessary to build a movement of committed Christian professors and staff on your campus. And we will give you opportunities to interact with other Faculty Affiliates and Christian Leadership Ministries staff in a variety of venues as we undertake to impact the university and the culture for the cause of Christ. One of the things that has attracted me and caused me to continue with Christian Leadership Ministries is the knowledge that I am investing my life in a magnificent cause. Can you imagine anything more challenging or rewarding than to impact all of higher education for the Master? Now that is something worth committing one's life to -- why don't you join us!

When Walter and I came on board with the faculty ministry of Campus Crusade for Christ in the late 1960s and early 1970s, things were a whole lot different than today. The application process was the same as for full-time Campus Crusade for Christ staff. We were required to attend the same three weeks of "New Staff" training that all Campus Crusade for Christ staff must complete, which included memorizing the *Four Spiritual Laws* and *God's Plan for Your Life*. We were expected to devote at least 10 percent of our time on the job to ministry activities -- which translated into about four to five hours per week of ministry, a pretty tough thing when you are trying to succeed in a demanding career. We were even supposed to fill out and turn in a weekly staff report detailing our activities. I don't think either Walter or I were very faithful to some of these requirements, which might explain why things are different now. We have carefully thought through the Faculty Affiliates program and structured it so that the emphasis is not on how much we can get out of you, but on how much Christian Leadership Ministries can support you as you go about your professional activities in the university and as you seek to represent Christ there as well. You may obtain additional information on the Faculty Affiliates program by contacting the Dallas office.

18. SPEAKING OPPORTUNITIES

When you consider how many universities and colleges there are in the U.S. alone and how we desire to have Christian faculty/staff ministries on most of them, you begin to get an idea of the enormous audience there is for talks on a variety of interesting themes. To be having the kind of impact we'd like to be having in the university, we would need to have hundreds of Christian professors and staff speaking every week on campuses around the country and around the world. Unfortunately, at the present time, there are only a very few who have seized upon this ministry opportunity. But when you consider the incredible impact these few are having, you wonder why more people don't begin to consider these options.

Walter Bradley has given his talk, "Scientific Evidence for the Existence of God" on scores of campuses to thousands of students, professors, and others -- usually to standing-room only crowds. Phil Johnson made a whirlwind tour last year to more than 25 campuses in this country and in Western Europe, speaking on the issues he raised in his book *Reason in the Balance*. Many of his appearances were sponsored by academic departments in the universities he visited. If Fritz Schaefer hasn't matched Walter Bradley with his talk "Stephen Hawking, God and the Big Bang" in terms of number of presentations and total audience, he can't be too far behind.

What is my point? Many professors and staff could be contributing in this important aspect of the battle for the university. Many of you have a research specialization or an intellectual interest in an area that would be of interest to others in academe. You just need to develop it into a presentation and start giving it. I remember when Walter first started developing his materials in the scientific evidence area. I sat in on an afternoon seminar he held in the Durrell Center at Colorado State University when he presented an early version of the talk. He has expanded the material over the years; he has added some good visuals; he has many more references and quotes. He started small at Texas A&M and gradually the opportunity grew. Ditto for Fritz Schaefer. We had him at Alabama on one of his first speaking jaunts. His talk has evolved, but it happened in progress as he traveled around and shared what he had.

One of the most frustrating things for me as we have traveled to dozens of universities and colleges is to hear someone say, "I've been meaning to put together a 'How to Make Better Grades' talk or I've thought about doing a position paper in my discipline and developing that into a talk, but I just haven't gotten around to it." We aren't going to win this thing with only a few in the fray! We need help. We need your help. I met a physics professor the other day at the University of North Texas, who has a goal of cranking out one apologetic talk each year and presenting his results as opportunities arise. As Howard Hendricks, a popular Christian speaker, says, "May his tribe increase!" If we could increase the number of individuals willing and prepared to minister in this way by an order of magnitude, we would still be way behind in terms of meeting the need.

If defending the faith against an angry mob in a public forum is not your idea of what the Lord has called you to, no problem. We need apologetic speakers, but we also need other kinds of speakers. We would like to see several hundred professors and staff members doing "How to Make Better Grades and Have More Fun" talks and "Time Management" talks. We would like to see professors doing position papers and talks. We just need talks, period. Can you help us? Start where you are with a topic on which you have some expertise. Develop a talk and start giving it on your own campus. Then look around for opportunities to take it on the road.

19. ORGANIZING FELLOWSHIPS

I never dreamed when I retired 2 1/2 years ago and went full time with Christian Leadership Ministries, that my job description, which I defined myself, would be "union organizer." But this is essentially what I do. I travel around the U.S. and the world organizing Christian Faculty/Staff Fellowships. The good news is that Peggy and I have visited more than 100 different campuses in our travels so far and we have challenged faculty and staff on each campus to begin a ministry. The bad news is that there are only 2,900 campuses left in the U.S. and about 1,990 campuses in other countries. We need help! We are running out of steam, so it will probably take about five more years to hit the next 100 campuses. Another impossible situation unless we can enlist some of you to become union organizers as you travel around on university business. There are two specific ways you can help in this respect.

When you visit other campuses in this country or overseas, check with our Dallas office to see whether there is anything going on there. If there is, read the chapter on Travel with a Purpose to see what to do. If there isn't, take that as an indication that you should try to get something started. If we have any contacts, get in touch with them and arrange to meet with them while you are on campus; if you arrive on the campus with no contacts, ask around, and you'll probably uncover some. If you have a Christian Faculty/Staff Fellowship or any kind of ministry activity on your campus, you qualify as an expert. It should be a simple thing for you to take a couple of copies of this manual along with you and share some of the concepts with your newfound Christian colleagues. Challenge them to get something started. You might offer to put them in touch with our ministry and continue to help them as necessary.

Another option that you might consider is to start a Christian group in your professional organization(s). As Christians, we need to be impacting our academic disciplines and one effective way of doing this is getting together with Christian colleagues within the discipline to discuss appropriate opportunities. You can be sure there are other groups within the discipline who are meeting together to push a common agenda -- the gays and lesbians are well-organized and well-entrenched in this respect, appearing in the official conference program and enjoying organizational funding and sponsorship in many professional organizations. If Christians aren't willing to take responsibility for setting agendas and policy in professional organizations, there are other groups who will. So consider becoming a "union organizer" in your professional organizations. One approach you might take as you step out in this way is to copy the chapter on the Christian Faculty/Staff Fellowship in this manual and get together with your Christian colleagues to discuss how the think tank approach could be modified to serve a role in the professional organization.

20. TRAVEL WITH A PURPOSE

I want to challenge you to change your mindset about travel. As I have mentioned, university and college people travel a lot, both within the U.S. and internationally. Whenever you make a work-related trip, think of it in terms of a possible ministry trip. Even if you are only going across the state to visit a neighboring campus, fruitful ministry opportunities might await you. Just put one additional item in your travel preparation checklist. Sometime in advance of your trip, call our Dallas office, inform them of your plans, and discuss with our headquarters staff how you might turn your business trip into a trip with eternal significance.

U.S. Travel

If your trip is within the U.S., ask the Christian Leadership Ministries staff whether there is a faculty/staff ministry in place where you are going. If not, you should go with the idea of trying to get something started as we have suggested. If there is already a Christian faculty/staff ministry in place, you should contact the leaders of the group to see whether there might be an opportunity for you to minister with them in some way. If you have developed a ministry talk (or talks), you probably will be in business. They might even be able to set you up with some professional appointments or speaking opportunities through local contacts in your academic discipline. At the very least, you could meet with the fellowship there and share with them your experience with the fellowship at your own university. You might share some innovative ideas you have tried at your school and you might learn some things from your hosts that you can take back to your group. I think there is a huge potential for this type of cross-fertilization and encouragement. It is certainly scriptural -- this is the focus of much of the book of Acts. We need to capitalize on opportunities we have in this regard. It won't happen if we don't become much more intentional.

International Travel

If your trip is an international trip, our staff will very likely work with you to arrange local contacts and ministry opportunities. Several years ago, Phil Bishop arranged to accompany one of his doctoral students to Quito, Ecuador, to help him collect data for his dissertation on altitude training of swimmers. Before he left, he contacted our Christian Leadership Ministries staff who coordinate our international ministry efforts, to let them know of his plans. Our staff contacted Campus Crusade for Christ's Latin American ministry headquarters, which quickly set Phil up with seven speaking engagements during his visit. Here is Phil's description of the trip.

"It was a wonderful ministry opportunity. The universities appeared Marxist-socialist in philosophy, but were quite willing to tolerate a succinct Gospel message in exchange for scientific lectures on metabolism, physiological psychology, and others. Many students I spoke to showed spiritual interest, and those attending filled out comment cards after each lecture. One of the attendees sent me this poignant message, '... thanks for giving me confidence that spiritual matters are more important. ... I will seek to walk the God road now.' One sows, another waters, and God causes the increase. It's always nice to do a little sowing."

"*Incidental* to a professional trip, I was able to participate in something eternally significant. God was able to use me to give Gospel presentations and encourage the Campus Crusade for Christ team in Quito. He also used the team to encourage me, and He strengthened my faith as well. ... As always, I gained more from the experience than those I went to help. Every trip we as Christian faculty make has the potential of reaping eternal benefits. God can use a small effort on our part to produce great results on His part."

In addition to professional trips that we initiate, we also have the opportunity to participate in international trips that are initiated by Christian Leadership Ministries. Since 1984, Christian Leadership Ministries has been sending teams of Christian professors and academic staff along with Christian Leadership Ministries staff on ministry/professional trips to other countries. The idea is to use professional-speaking opportunities as an entree to ministry. In the summer of 1984, Peggy and I along with Stan Oakes (the director of Christian Leadership), Mike Duggins (the Christian Leadership staff representative in Texas), Walter and Ann Bradley, Jim Stock (University of South Florida), Duane Keilstrup (University of Texas Arlington), Jim Henderson (Baylor), Bob McGowan (Memphis State University), Dick Stealey (Ball State University), and Bill Floyd (University of Wisconsin-La Crosse) made that first trip to South Africa. For many of us, it was our first international experience. For the country of South Africa, it was the beginning of a faculty ministry movement that is still in existence. Jim Stock has returned regularly to South Africa since then using professional contacts he established to fund ongoing ministry involvement in the country.

Since that first trip, Christian Leadership Ministries has sent dozens of teams into many countries including: Kenya, Thailand, Japan, Singapore, Korea, Hong Kong, the former Soviet Union, Poland, Latvia, Romania, and a host of others. Let me share with you the kind of impact we as professors and academic staff can have if we are willing to travel professionally and let the Lord use us in ministry activity as we go. Some years ago on a trip to Europe, Peggy and I met a young missionary couple from a closed country. The man was interested to learn that our ministry frequently sends university professors on international trips to open ministry doors, and he promptly invited us to bring a team to his country. Frankly, we hadn't thought at all about visiting that country, and it really wasn't very high on our list of travel places, but he was so sincerely interested in having us come and so optimistic about what such a trip might do for his ministry, we agreed to bring a team. We asked around our Christian Leadership Ministries contacts to see whether any other professors or staff would be willing to accompany us. Apparently, they all felt the same way we did because there were no takers.

So the following summer, Peggy and I set out to spend 10 days with him in his country. He had set me up with two professional talks in two different universities in the country, and we had one meeting with several government officials. That was it, not very much in comparison with some of the trips we have made where we are speaking several times a day. We had a wonderful time in the country. It was beautiful; quite different from our American idea of what we would find. The presentations went well, and so did the meeting. But there was no spiritual content whatsoever to anything I said or did. There could not be. I remember remarking to Peggy on the way home that we had wasted a lot of our time and money and didn't really have too much to show for our efforts. That was before we heard back from our missionary.

He wrote me later that he had been able to use the contacts he had made at my presentations and the meeting with the officials to develop a ministry focus that has connected him at the very highest levels of the leadership of the country. When I read the letter, the details of which I can't disclose, I saw the sovereign hand of God working through our feeble efforts to accomplish His desired ends in that land. It was absolutely miraculous. Never in my wildest imaginations could I have pictured what He was able to accomplish from our visit. And it is a good thing. I would have been so proud of myself! As it turned out, all I could do was shake my head and say, "God did it all and to Him be the glory!" Our responsibility in all of this is to go; God is entirely responsible for the results.

One final comment on this. We originally started international trips with a view toward training and equipping Christian professors and staff within countries to carry on ministry activity after we left. When the former Soviet Union began to open up, we moved more to using professional-speaking opportunities to generate evangelistic contacts for Christian ministry workers within the country. More recently, we have moved back closer to our original objective. What is exciting about this, however, is the opportunity for long-term relationships in a particular country and something we are just starting to see -- the opportunity for a Christian Faculty/Staff Fellowship in the U.S. to focus on a long-term relationship with a particular country. Mike Sorgius, our

Christian Leadership Ministries representative at the University of Florida, has been leading faculty/staff teams to Mongolia for several years. This spring, Mike took a team of six or seven University of Florida faculty and staff to Mongolia. This is exciting. This is intentional. This will accelerate Christian efforts in Mongolia and encourage the fellowship at the University of Florida.

Change your mindset about travel. Every time you start packing your bags for a professional trip, think ministry.

"They traveled to and fro across the land, and knowledge increased." Did you get the message? There are unparalleled ministry opportunities waiting for you just beyond the boundaries of your university. If you are not already participating with us nationally and internationally, pray as Jabez did saying, "Oh, that You would bless me, and enlarge my border." 1 Chronicles 4:10 And then start looking for ways you can help us establish faculty/staff ministries in other universities and in other lands.

PART FOUR:

REGRETS

Of the talks I am presenting as we travel around the United States and the world with Christian Leadership, the most frequently requested by a wide margin is "Regrets Upon Completing Twenty-five Years in Academia." It is fairly obvious to me why this topic is so popular with university professors and staff. You see, each of us is a bit nervous about the way we invest our time and live our life. It is comforting to hear someone else voice his regrets on completing a particular stage in life and to be able to say, "Oh, I've already got that covered." At least, this is what I suspect is the motivation for the interest. Unfortunately, or fortunately, depending on your perspective, the regrets I share in the talk are likely to be the very ones many professors or staff members would bring up at the end of a career in the academy, and I have seen little evidence that more than a few individuals would have these concerns covered.

My regrets have nothing much to do with the professional side of my career. On the contrary, I had a wonderful 25 years at the University of Alabama. The university was very, very good to me and for me. For most of my tenure at the university, I was the senior faculty member in my area. I taught pretty much what I wanted to teach when I wanted to teach it. My research flourished, I believe, as a consequence of my having committed it early on to the Lord. I was fortunate to have generated approximately $1.25 million in sponsored research funding during a time in which this type of funding was unheard of for business school professors. Thus, I had funds for research assistants, travel, and equipment that most of my colleagues did not have. I was also blessed with connections, mostly former students, who enabled me to do research and consult with some of the most prestigious organizations in the country -- AT&T, General Motors, and NASA to name a few. In the early 1980s, I made a mid-career shift in my research, moving into the area of using artificial intelligence methods in the design of complex manufacturing and communication systems -- which was also unusual for a business professor. For the last 15 or so years I taught almost exclusively graduate students, mostly my own students, in very small classes. And during that time, I chaired more than 20 doctoral dissertations. For most of my career, I was well-paid by the university and was able to cash in on a very generous retirement situation after completing 25 years of service. All in all, I had a very satisfying career. You could say that I had it made.

What, then, were my regrets? Well, the things I regret about my time at the university are concerned with models, ministry, and methods. Let me explain.

Looking back over my career, I think the most difficult aspect of it was there were no role models for me to follow. I was not fortunate as a graduate student to be mentored in how to succeed in the university; consequently, I pretty much had to discover this by trial and error. I didn't have a clue how to develop a research program and how to go about the important task of generating refereed publications. I did have good incentive, thanks to a former dean who called me into his office early in my career and gave me the best professional advice I ever got, "Rae, you are not going to be promoted this year and you will never be promoted as long as I'm dean of this college until you start doing research and having it published." Pretty direct. No sugar-coating here at all! Yet, the man did me a huge favor and I look at that conversation as a real turning point in my life. This is why the tenure workshops I have encouraged you to consider are so vital. We have an unusual opportunity to help young Christian and non-Christian professors succeed in the university.

But my concern about role models goes much deeper than this. For me, there were *no* models of what it was to be a Christian professor. What is a Christian professor? What does one look like? What does one do? What differentiates a Christian professor from any other professor or from a professor who just happens to be a Christian? Many times in my career, I would have welcomed the chance to just look over at Dr. Christian, Professor of Engineering or Professor of History, who was a model of what I needed to become: someone who was succeeding in his teaching and research and who was having an impact for Christ on the institution and on his students and colleagues; someone who had it together in his family and in his church; someone who was respected as a Christian man or woman in the university, in the church, and in the community. There was no one. To be sure, there were professors who were involved in their church -- but not visible on campus. There were Christians who were successful in the academy, but they were "Secret Service" Christians as far as the university was concerned. Looking back on my early years, I can't think of a single professor who was making a strong stand for Christ on campus.

So one of the things I wanted to accomplish in my career was to be an example of what a Christian professor is to younger professors and staff, and older ones, too, if they were interested. I haven't always been all that I could. I have not taken advantage of all the opportunities I had. I have not always been as bold as I should have been or wanted to be. I would do things differently if I could start all over again knowing what I know now. I think I could be much more effective the second time around. Regardless of what I have been able to *do* on my own and challenging others to work with me, I have always tried to *be* a Christian professor. And I can say with a degree of satisfaction, "You want to know what a Christian professor is? I'm a Christian professor. You follow me as I follow Christ, and I think you will learn something of what it means to be a Christian and a professor." So one of my regrets is there were no models. Hopefully, you won't have this same regret; there are many Christian professors in academia now, with more coming along each year. People like Walter Bradley, Phil Bishop, Byron Johnson, Jim Stock, Larry Caillouet and a host of others; who challenge me with their commitment to the Master and to changing the university for Him. These are people who can challenge you. There are probably some on your own campus.

A second regret I had as I reached the end of my career as a professor had to do with ministry, or rather the ministry, more specifically, with Christian Leadership Ministries, the faculty ministry of Campus Crusade for Christ. When we first became involved with Campus Crusade for Christ, there was a faculty ministry. When we were challenged to join Campus Crusade for Christ as Associate Staff, we were told there were about 25 other faculty couples around the country who were also on Associate Staff. This was a strong incentive for us to join -- I saw our involvement as one way I could find models of Christian professors. So in July of 1972, Peggy, Jonathan, Jennifer, and I flew to California to go through staff training subsequent to joining the faculty ministry.

Interestingly, shortly after we "came on staff" as it was called, the faculty ministry started to evaporate. Jim Engel, a Professor of

Marketing at Ohio State University who had started the ministry, worked heroically to keep things together, but he was fighting a losing battle. He was trying to have a career in academia, which meant all of the teaching and research and committee work, as well as trying to run a national ministry at the same time. It simply couldn't be done. So by about 1975, the faculty ministry was basically gone. Walter and Ann Bradley and Peggy and I continued our relationship with Campus Crusade for Christ working primarily with the student ministry or with other projects that came down the Campus Crusade for Christ pike such as the "I've Found It!" campaign and the *JESUS* film. I recall a conversation I had with Dr. Bill Bright, president and founder of Campus Crusade for Christ, in early 1976. I was doing a sabbatical at the Massachusetts Institute of Technology and had flown from Cambridge to Chicago for a training session for the "I've Found It!" campaign. I rode back to the airport from the conference hotel with Dr. Bright and he commented that if he could start Campus Crusade for Christ all over again, he would pay a lot more attention to professors.

Well, in 1980, Dr. Bright determined to restart the faculty ministry -- this time with much more in the way of resources than in the days when Jim Engel was a one-man-show. He challenged Stan Oakes to give leadership to the new effort and provided other full time staff and funding to do what was necessary to get the job done. The rest is history. As I have mentioned, we started with some regional meetings around the country that Walter Bradley and I participated in, and gradually, the ministry became what it is today -- 100 full-time staff, about 12,000 Christian professors and staff on almost every college and university campus in this country and around the world, and an expanding array of ministry tools and resources. Seventeen years down the road, we have made tremendous strides from our early beginnings. And we have a strategy to impact all of higher education that is well under way.

I regret that for the first dozen years of my career at the university, there was no national ministry organization with which I could connect, for vision, for resources, for relationships, for strategy. There simply was nothing. From 1974 to 1980, Walter and Ann and Peggy and I met every other year in Fort Collins, Colorado, at Campus Crusade for Christ's summer staff training, and that was basically my connection with Christian professors in the world! What I would give to be able to relive those years having Christian Leadership Ministries in Dallas available to me -- with all it has to offer. I am pretty sure I could have been much more effective as a Christian professor if that was possible. But it is not, at least, not for me. But Christian Leadership Ministries is available for you, to come alongside and help you succeed as a Christian professor or staff member in the university. And for that, I am glad. Take advantage of a huge opportunity that we did not have. Plug in to Christian Leadership Ministries. Use it to accomplish your goals at your university. Help it with your involvement, your prayers, and your financial support.

My final regret has to do with methods. When we first began thinking about reaching out as professors in the university, there were no methods. There was no strategy. There was nothing. When I first started meeting with colleagues on the University of Alabama campus, Christian Leadership Ministries was eight years in the future. In a very real sense, we have had to invent everything we did in the ministry: the Faculty/Staff Fellowship, the *Real Issue*, tenure workshops, position papers, Worldwide Web home pages, everything. Many professors, staff members and Christian Leadership Ministries staff, have contributed in this respect for a long time. In fact, we are still inventing. That is the nature of the ministry, and if we ever stop inventing, we are dead -- the Faculty/Staff Fellowship must be a research and development activity if it is to effectively impact the university.

I can remember strategy sessions at our Christian Leadership Ministries staff training in the early years, talking about how we desperately needed more bullets in our arsenal. And we would try to identify what the logical next steps might be and who we had who could give attention to that area. At one of those meetings, Walter and I determined to try to develop some "How To" materials. During the next months, we wrote what became known as the *Faculty Impact* series. At another meeting, we talked about needing help in the legal issues area, and over the next year or so, Scott Luley put together the excellent video workshop we have in the *Freedom of Expression* arena. Some of our best tools have happened almost serendipitously as individuals have tried to reach out in new and different ways. And we have had some colossal failures, too. Our freshmen orientation at which we had 30 Christian professors and staff and only four freshmen is one example. Walter Bradley shares a wonderful story of how he and Ann invited all of their friends on the faculty when he was at the Colorado School of Mines to an outreach at their apartment. Through no fault of theirs, the affair degenerated into a shouting match that lasted forever and, Walter thought he was ruined professionally.

I could go on in this vein for a long time. I won't. But how often I would like to redo my career knowing, what I know now about ministry. I regret that I only learned how to reach out to students in such an attractive way as the "How to Make Better Grades and Have More Fun" format toward the end of my career. Sometimes, I'd like to go back and do it all over again. I regret that I was only just beginning to learn how to reach out to colleagues effectively with *The Seven Habits of Highly Effective People* material as I neared retirement. I'd like to go back and do that over again. I can't. But you have access to these and many other strategies and resources. Take advantage of them! They are yours for the asking through Christian Leadership Ministries.

You will have regrets at the end of your career. I don't think they will be much about your professional accomplishments. I have not once since leaving academia wished that I could have another refereed journal article published. I don't think you will either. I haven't once wished I could deliver another of my sterling lectures to a rapt group of students. I don't think you will either. I think your regrets will be similar to mine -- that you were not as effective for the Savior in the university as you might have been. What will you say the problem was? No models? No Christian Leadership Ministry? No methods? I hope not. In fact, I think that if you will faithfully begin to incorporate some of the ideas I have suggested here, on an individual basis, and working together with your colleagues, you might have *no regrets*. Perhaps you will even decide to come join Christian Leadership Ministries full-time working with professors and staff to change the university for the Lord Jesus Christ!